THE RIGHT OF THE CATECHIZED
TO THE TRUTH

The Right of the Catechized to the Truth

The Cardinal Oddi Catechetical Day

Sponsored by the
Notre Dame Pontifical Catechetical Institute
Arlington, Virginia

and

nine more talks
given in the United States
July 8, 1983—July 16, 1983

ST. PAUL EDITIONS

Cover Credit: DSP

ISBN 0-8198-6407-2

Copyright © 1984, by the Daughters of St. Paul

Printed in the U.S.A., by the Daughters of St. Paul
50 St. Paul's Ave., Boston, MA 02130

The Daughters of St. Paul are an international congregation of Women Religious serving the Church with the communications media.

CONTENTS

Foreword	11
Unity Is Our Strength	13
Good Texts, Good Teachers	17
The Right of the Catechized to the Truth	21
The Truth and "Pluralism"	37
Introduction to the Panel	41
The Call of Catholic Parents for Organic and Systematic Catechetical Teaching	43
The Place and Role of Memory as a God-given Natural Power, Especially Significant in the Formative Years of Childhood	49
The Bishop and the Handing On of the Faith	57
The Importance of the Elements of Christian Doctrine	63
The Good Samaritan	71
Living and Teaching Christ	75
Bring Light into Darkness	79
The Holy Year and Reconciliation	83
The Respective Rights of the Family, Church and State in the Education of the Child	87

FOREWORD

Silvio Cardinal Oddi is the Prefect of the Sacred Congregation for the Clergy, one of the most important organs at Rome which serves the Successor of St. Peter in his government of the Universal Church. Contained within this Congregation is the Pope's Office for Catechetics. Cardinal Oddi received his appointment to this post of high responsibility from the present Holy Father, succeeding the late well-remembered Cardinal John Wright.

Cardinal Oddi has had a distinguished career in the service of the Holy See of St. Peter. Included among the scenes of his apostolic work were Cairo in Egypt, Jerusalem in the Holy Land, and Belgium. Catholics who remember happily and well the good Pope John XXIII will recognize a special dimension in the personality of Cardinal Oddi deriving from the fact that he served as Secretary to Cardinal Roncalli during his years at Paris as Papal Nuncio to France.

Most Reverend Thomas J. Welsh, since transferred to Allentown, invited Cardinal Oddi to come for a "Cardinal Oddi Catechetical Day" on July 9, 1983, sponsored by Notre Dame Institute, the Pontifical Catechetical Institute located in the Diocese of Arlington, Virginia. The book presented here contains the message of the Day itself, together with the extension of this fundamental catechetical message in further discourses of the Cardinal at New York, Detroit and Boston.

What is this catechetical message? The title of the thematic discourse, chosen by Cardinal Oddi, puts it with truly Roman brevity and clarity: "The Right of the Catechized to the Truth." Close students of *Catechesi tradendae* will recognize that Cardinal Oddi speaks for Pope John Paul II. Cardinal Ratzinger put the same catechetical message of the Holy See into a similar application earlier this year in France.

It is an honor for this Pontifical Catechetical Institute to have had Cardinal Oddi for this occasion, and to work toward that good fruit which the "Cardinal Oddi Catechetical Day" will surely bear for the children of the People of God in America.

Eugene Kevane

August 15, 1983
Feast of the Assumption

Unity Is Our Strength

Remarks of Silvio Cardinal Oddi to the Priests of Arlington, Virginia, 4:00 p.m., Friday, July 8, 1983.

My dear Brothers in Christ and fellow Priests of the Diocese of Arlington:

It is a special pleasure for me to meet you here, particularly now that I know who your new Bishop is. You surely know that it was Bishop Welsh who originally invited me to come to Arlington to talk and, after he was transferred to the larger Diocese of Allentown, I wondered whether it would be proper for me to visit the diocese *sede vacante*.

But when I heard that Bishop Keating was named successor and so many good things were said about him in Rome, my uncertainties disappeared and here I am!

I must confess that it never seems like work for me to meet priests. I liked to meet priests long before I was appointed to my present job as Prefect of the Sacred Congregation for the Clergy. I enjoy the feeling of ease that comes over me in the presence of priests, that *camaraderie* that prevails among us. I know that some of us can be a little stuffy and some a little rough, but we have an enormous amount in common, regardless of where we were born or what language we speak.

We were all chosen by God, educated in the same type of school with the same subjects. We all live to serve the Church in one way or another. Most of us prefer to do pastoral work with the people rather than attend meetings where superiors spend half their lives. We share the secrets of countless hearts. We tell the same stories, which few outside our fraternity appreciate. We daily offer the same Sacrifice. People habitually think we are better than we are. We have a lot in common, but I feel particularly at home among you because, in addition to all the above, you enjoy the reputation of remaining loyal and faithful to the Holy See even in these difficult times.

One of the things that has concerned me over recent years is the tendency among priests in some quarters to spend the majority of their free time with lay men and women rather than with fellow priests. I think that is unfortunate because we need each other.

I offer no hard and fast rule on this subject, but the fact is that all my life, though a diocesan priest from Piacenza, I have tried to live in communities of priests and have usually been able to find one. I have been comforted, helped and inspired by the priests with whom I have been privileged to live over the decades. I mix, of course, daily with laity, receiving them at my office and at home, socializing with them at diplomatic and other receptions with which Rome is replete, accepting occasional invitations to dine out. All this is necessary and good, but I find myself desirous of seeking relaxation among fellow priests.

I can talk freely among them. I do not have to explain and excuse myself. They understand what I am trying to say. They are my brothers, and one is always at home with one's brothers.

I have no message for you today. I just wanted to meet my brothers in Arlington. This year I celebrated the Golden Anniversary of ordination to the Priesthood. A month ago one of the men in my office took it upon himself to arrange for all the priests in my office and for me to concelebrate early morning Mass with the Holy Father. There were twenty-one of us altogether. There was no sermon, no prayer of the faithful, but I felt deeply the unity of the priesthood that day. Young and old, strong and weak, high and low, each one of us is a *Sacerdos in aeternum.* As that mysterious Melchizedek of old prefigured the High Priest to come, unaware of his exalted mission though he was, so we who carry on the Priesthood of Jesus continue to offer the Sacrifice of the Son of God as a foretaste of the Eternal Banquet in the presence of the Lamb, though we still only understand in a dark manner the sublime nature of our divine calling.

Each one of us is a special copy of the Eternal Priest. Our individual differences blend into that priestly character with which our souls were stamped on the day of our ordination. The people like to see us as priests, to be able to recognize us, to be proud of us, and I think this is particularly true here in the United States. I am impressed by the number of people who salute me, not because I am a prelate—they seldom know that—but because I am a priest.

One day I overheard a visiting priest in my office ask one of my staff: "Do you have a lot of problems sent in?"

"Yes," my staff member replied, "but I'm glad about that. *Se tutta va bene, siamo rovinati.*" (If everything goes well, we are out of work!)

So, take courage. Until original sin is proved not to exist, things will continue to go badly. So we priests need never fear to be out of work.

Good Texts, Good Teachers

Remarks of Silvio Cardinal Oddi on the occasion of a visit to the offices of the Department of Religious Education of the National Catholic Education Association, Washington, D.C., on Friday, July 8, 1983.

It is a great satisfaction for me to have been invited by Father Francis Kelly to meet you here personally and to get to know some of the people on whom the catechetical apostolate in the United States depends for its vitality, organization and even inspiration. It is a consolation for me to know that Father Kelly wished me to meet you because we are engaged in the same work of spreading the Word of God, and I am strengthened by the knowledge that we are working together.

I am not going to make a speech, but I do want to take advantage of being here to share a few thoughts with you, pertinent to our joint apostolate.

First of all, I wish to thank you. I have been following your work as reflected in your monthly bulletin and through the conversations which I have had with Father Kelly on his visits to Rome. I am deeply impressed by your professional competence and the zeal which you put into your labors for the faith. For the most part your work is a hidden one, but it is extremely important. Everyone hopes, of course, that the current shortage of dedicated teaching Sisters will prove short-lived, but until the day when their numbers increase to former levels, teaching the faith to the young will become a bigger and bigger challenge. Yours is the task to find new ways to reach the young no longer taught by Sisters. Parents, above all, lay teachers, parish catechists—and do not forget priests—must be found and trained to take up the slack and you are in an excellent position to make that search and to organize the training of newly recruited pastoral workers to teach the faith, always, it goes without saying, under the Hierarchy.

Second, it is common knowledge, as Cardinal Ratzinger said in Paris not too many weeks ago, that contentless catechisms are one of the major problems in today's catechetical apostolate. This is a problem which must be explored and solved, and my office has done some preliminary work on it already. I hope that you, also, are investigating ways to improve current catechetical texts from the point of view of doctrinal and moral content.

There is no question in my mind that we need reliable and complete catechetical texts according to the age and condition of the respective catechumens, but more important than the text, much more important, is the teacher, the catechist. After all, Jesus Himself, the Apostles and most all catechists until the birth of Gutenberg taught without the help of catechisms for individual catechumens, and nevertheless the faith was spread throughout the world.

A well-prepared, devout catechist, who practices what he or she is preaching, is essential to the success of any catechetical instruction. It is not a question of "either a good catechism, or a good teacher," it is a question of both. Sometimes the publishers of content-less catechisms defend them by saying that they are intended for use by good teachers who will supplement them. The difficulty is, however, that oftentimes the teachers themselves have been prepared with content-less or inadequate texts and are thus unable to fill in the lacunae for their own charges.

I urge you, therefore, to give thought to improving the preparation of teachers. Catechetical Institutes would, of course, be the natural vehicle, but the nature of such an institute is of prime importance. It will serve little if it dedicates an exaggerated amount of time to methodology and ignores the principal task of communicating what Christ teaches through His Church.

My third point flows from the coincidence that I happened to receive Father Kelly's invitation to visit you on the feast of the Nativity of St. John the Baptist. The role of the catechist is similar to the role of the Baptist—to prepare people to receive the Christ. Most of the people whom catechists instruct in this country of yours have already been baptized. Their souls have been stamped with the Christian character. But, at the same time, most of them know little about Jesus as yet. It is the catechist's job to make Jesus a living Person for them and to lead them to a closer and closer union with Him. It is through the catechist's voice that catechumens will be led to penetrate ever more deeply their relationship to the Son of God.

John was a voice crying in the wilderness. What did he cry, his own ideas? No, he announced the Word, the Word that was from the beginning. The catechist, too, is a voice that preaches the Word of God, not his or her own message. Of course, John had his own effective style of announcing the Word and his personal asceticism arrested the attention of many, but the Word that came to be known through his voice was the authentic Word, undiluted by the personality or the reasoning of the Baptist.

Part of your job, also, must be to take steps to insure, insofar as your position permits, that the catechists, in whose remote preparation you have a part, are faithful voices transmitting not their own message but the Word of God. To do this they themselves must be inspired by that Word and be seen to live by it.

It has been a pleasure to be able to meet you, and I hope that when you come to Rome you will not fail to visit me. May God bless you all.

The Right of the Catechized to the Truth

Address of Silvio Cardinal Oddi, Prefect of the Sacred Congregation for the Clergy, in Arlington, Virginia, July 9, 1983.

If I were given the opportunity to choose an area to visit in the United States around the Fourth of July, I would probably pick Virginia—the site of the first permanent English settlement of what was to become your United States of America. As it happened, I did not have the opportunity to choose, but Divine Providence did, through the Diocese of Arlington and Msgr. Eugene Kevane of the Notre Dame Institute in Middleburg. So, here I am, though a few days late for the fireworks, which on the other hand may follow what I have to say.

I have been invited, as you well know, to speak on a subject which falls under my responsibility in the government of the Church as Prefect of the Sacred Congregation for the Clergy, and which, by its very nature, is of intense interest to you as catechists or parents dedicated to transmitting the faith to those under your charge, namely, the subject of catechetics.

Catechesis is the art of maturing initial faith and educating true disciples of Christ.[1] In this strict sense of the term it is the process of making a more explicit personal attachment to Jesus, the Truth (Jn. 14:6), after baptism. But the word catechetics is used also in a wider sense and, taken together with all its implications, it is an extensive subject indeed. So, I have decided to limit myself to one aspect of it, an aspect which, it seems to me, is timely in this age which loves pluralism in its every manifestation: "The Right of the Catechized to the Truth."

At first glance, this declaration may seem as self-evident as the phrase on the American dollar, "In God We Trust." Everyone, not only Americans, must trust in God, and everyone, not only the catechized, has the right to the truth. The fact is, however, as we well know, not everyone trusts in God, nor is everyone's right to the truth honored. So, in the area of catechesis, it is necessary to examine the right of every man, woman and child to hear the truth about God, and the corollary of this right, the obligation of the Church to insure that God's truth is faithfully communicated.

In missionary countries, one who is striving to deepen his or her initial faith is often called a catechumen. But those who have not even been baptized and are meeting the doctrine of the faith for the first time are also called catechumens. In the older local Churches we even speak of "adult catechetics," "catechism for adults," and other such phrases which reveal that in popular usage, the word catechetics is employed to indicate passing on the Word of God at almost any level to almost any age group, to baptized as well as aspirants to baptism. Hence, in this broad sense, we are all catechumens, you and I, just as much as the Korean housewife meeting Jesus for the first time. Let us look, then, at what we have a right to be taught.

Four Marks of Truth

In your remarkable Baltimore Catechism, published originally over a century ago, and responsible in no small part for the theological formation, the fidelity and sanctity of the Church in this country, Americans learned that the four marks of the Church are: unity, holiness, catholicity and apostolicity.[2] This is still true and always will be. The Church is one, not many; she is holy, not sinful; she is universal, not national; she is apostolic in direction and not guided by private interpretation.

It seems to me that these same four marks are, with the proper adaptation, characteristic also of truth, and I would like to examine each one of them in that regard. My treatment of them, however, will not be equal, in the sense that equal time will be given to each, because I shall devote most of the time available to a consideration of the first mark, the unity and integrity of truth, as a necessary sign of authentic doctrine, and as an aid to clarifying the nature of permitted pluralism.

Part of the American cultural and moral heritage is your respect for a man's word. One tends to find that a man's word here is truly his bond. This presumption that one tells the truth is reinforced also in the oath which witnesses take in your courts to bind themselves before God to tell the truth, and not only the truth but "the truth, the whole truth and nothing but the truth." Even on the civil level, the integrity of the truth is revered among you. For a statement to be considered true in your courts, it must contain the full truth and remain free of falsehood. If it is not integrally true or if it contains error along with truth, it is not good enough for judge and jury. *A fortiori,* incomplete statements about the faith, or statements of the truth combined with erroneous matter are not good enough for those studying the Word of God.

If you will forgive me a moment of pedantry, I should like to make this point stronger by calling your attention to the Greek word for truth. It is *alétheia*. Now the Greek word *létheia* means *"forgetting."* When it is preceded by alpha privitive (a), it means "truth," that is, *not forgetting*.

For the Greeks, too, to the fathers of logic, telling the truth meant not forgetting, not leaving out anything that should be there.

If an essential aspect of a statement is omitted, therefore, regardless of how much truth it may hold, the statement is false, as not a few students have discovered to their chagrin when taking true and false examinations.

Let me offer a few examples of how this principle should govern catechetics. If we teach the catechumen that Jesus was born of Mary of Nazareth but do not specify that she was a virgin (Lk. 1:27), our teaching is not true because it is not complete, it does not contain the whole truth. The virginity of Mary is an essential element of the divine economy which redeemed mankind through the Incarnation of the Second Person of the Blessed Trinity. If Jesus had not been conceived of a virgin, His father would have been human. But we know that it was the Holy Spirit Who "overshadowed" Mary (Lk. 1:35). The virginity of Mary is, then, a necessary background for the avenue the Almighty chose to effect our salvation.

Jesus is both true God and true Man (Nicene Creed). He was tempted and suffered for us,[3] which only as Man was He capable of doing. He was able to atone for our sins, which only as the Eternal Word of God (Jn. 1:1) was He capable of achieving, so what we say or do not say about the Virgin Mother of God must be consonant with other essential doctrines of our faith. Good Christology is also good Mariology.

If we teach that Jesus was the most perfect Man that ever lived, we rightly emphasize His humanity and His sinlessness and thus are able to explain to our students that Jesus understands what man is, and that they themselves, with His help, are capable of resisting temptation and imitating His loving example. But we must simultaneously emphasize that He is also God (Jn. 8:58), for otherwise the Redemption becomes logically and theologically impossible and Christianity collapses. Unless He is God, Jesus is incapable of reconciling man with His Father.

Deficient Doctrine Proposed

Too many catechumens today, however, are receiving only a part of the doctrine of faith. There is a veritable antipathy in some quarters against catechetical texts that state unequivocally the doctrine of faith. This may be why young people are neglecting their religious duties, as correspondence coming into my office from some parts of the world informs that they are. It is clear that, if we teach only that the Apostles saw Jesus after His death, but do not mention the graphic details of His eating broiled fish (Lk. 24:42), nor the invitation to Thomas to put a fist into the divine side (Jn. 20:27), nor the meeting of Mary Magdalene who at first did not recognize Him—so unprepared was she for His return (Jn. 20:14), then the catechized are being denied their right to the whole truth. Why is this so? Because we are leaving them exposed to current half-truths about the bodily resurrection of Christ which, in a laudable effort to avoid exaggeration in Scriptural interpretation, give, in effect, a distorted view of the Gospel story, and deprive the student of a full picture of the resurrection of Christ. The whole truth is, of course, that the Apostles did not hallucinate. Jesus rose from the dead in fact, body and soul, was seen by many, ate with some, convinced even those who at first doubted that it was He, and subsequently ascended into heaven. No hallucinations at all: reality (cf. Acts 10:40-43).

What fundamentally is truth? Pilate was troubled by the same question and philosophers through the ages have grappled with it. Truth is the conformity of the mind to external reality. Truth demands, therefore, submission to some reality outside oneself, and this is the rub. Man wants to establish what is true and what is not all by himself, without reference to anything or anyone outside of him; we remain sons of Adam, heirs of his deviant self-centered propensities. But truth is not, of course, determined by personal opinion; it rests on objective reality. Not far from this spot, as a matter of fact, Pope John Paul II defined truth as "a surrender to reality."[4]

We are called upon always to make this surrender to truth, particularly to Divine Truth, but often, like Pilate, we cynically try to avoid it or even, like Satan, stand in blatant rebellion, moved by a pride that will yield neither to man nor to God. Some religious truths are not easy to accept, either because they demand a curbing of strong human instinct or because our limited reason is too weak to grasp them, but God expects acceptance anyway, the acceptance of faith. We remember how Jesus looked sadly after those who left Him when He told the crowds He would give them the Eucharist—His flesh to eat and His Blood to drink. Some found it a "hard saying" and walked away (Jn. 6:60), but Peter and the Apostles stayed with Him, as we must also.

Revealed truth is not something we arrive at by reason, but by faith. It is the will that must push the reason to accept, not because the concept is totally understood by the mind, but because God has revealed it and we trust Him. The young must be taught to study the doctrine of the Church through eyes of faith, and they must be taught what God has revealed, which, it goes without saying, is much more important than what they themselves are able to deduce from the analysis of a dramatic picture in a textbook.

Catechists, therefore, must be extremely careful not to censure the Word of God. God has not taught man anything that will hurt him. Anyone who attempts to block the march of the innocent toward the full truth is destroying the child's very reason for existence and contradicting the very purpose of the Incarnation: to rescue man from the father of lies and present him to the Father of Truth. By making man and woman to His likeness (Gn. 1:26), God gave every human being the right to the truth, that is, to a knowledge of Him as He is, undistorted by human attempts to reduce the Creator to the level of creature.

There is, naturally, the corresponding obligation among those charged with the formation of the young to respect the right of their charges to the truth, the whole truth and nothing but, carefully distinguishing the teaching of the Church from human opinion. Our present Holy Father bluntly reminded teachers of religion: "Theologians and exegetes have a duty to take great care that people do not take for a certainty what, on the contrary, belongs to the area of questions of opinion or discussions among the experts.... (Catechists) must refuse to trouble the minds of the young at this (early) stage of their catechesis with outlandish theories, useless questions and unproductive discussions, things that St. Paul often condemned in his pastoral letters."[5]

Minds Opened, To Close on Something

Some teachers of religion today seem to spend more time giving their charges exercises in "reading readiness" than on teaching them solid doctrine. Good teachers do not spend the entire class getting children interested, leaving little time to get across the matter at hand. Possibly the teacher is not at fault, but the person who prepared a syllabus devoid of content. The Trinity cannot be mentioned because the child will not understand it. Sin cannot be mentioned because the child will acquire a guilt complex. Hell cannot be mentioned because the child will be traumatized. The evil of divorce cannot be mentioned because so many of the child's relatives are divorced. Possibly pictures, films and discussions have become necessary to fill in the time unoccupied by a presentation of the Word of God. But, once opened, the little mind must be given something substantial on which to close. No catechist has the right to deny the child knowledge of the fundamentals of the faith. A teacher unable to teach about the Fall, the Redemption, sin, grace, judgment, heaven and hell without traumatizing his or her pupils is not worthy of his or her salt. Sometimes children are taught at too early an age things it would be better if they did *not* know, while at the same time being denied knowledge of things they *should* know at *every* age.

Do not become alarmed, my friends; I have not fallen into a currently stylish fundamentalism, forgetting: "Love one another just as I have loved you" (Jn. 13:34) or, "In my Father's house there are many mansions" (Jn. 14:2). But can one understand the Hail Mary without knowing what sin is? All I am asking is that the child be given the full Gospel and taught all ten of the commandments, for no one can love God without knowing in what the love of God consists: "If you love me, keep my commandments" (Jn. 14:15). The mild, beloved, short-lived Pope John Paul I chose to tell the Bishops of the Philippines on the last day of his life: "One of the greatest rights of the faithful is to receive the Word of God in all its purity and *integrity*."[6]

There are, of course, many areas of theology and biblical studies where the truth may not be clear to the human mind and on which the Church has not pronounced. Here a pluralism of opinion is acceptable in the proper forum, but even here pluralism has its limits. An opinion cannot be true if it contradicts a certainty. The philosophers warn: *non est negandum notum propter ignotum.* One may not deny the known in order to discover the unknown. If a denial of what the Church holds as certain is necessary to unlock a "new truth," where does that take us? Obviously, the "new truth" is false. So any given phrase of Scripture or the Magisterium must be interpreted, not in isolation, but in the context of the entire deposit of faith.

Truth Is Holy

We now move on to the second mark of truth; it is holy. Truth is holy because God is Truth. "I am the truth," Jesus told us (Jn. 14:6). Nothing that is true is a threat to the dignity, to the sanctification of man. Everything that God has done and has made is intended for man's sanctification if used by man according to the demands of his nature and according to divine teaching. Our bodies, nature in general, and scientific discoveries are all good in themselves. The evaluation of the morality of their use, however, depends on whether or not a particular use contributes to realizing the purpose for which God created man.

The Church is not afraid of truth, any kind of truth, because God *is* Truth, but at the same time the circumstances of imparting truth to the young must be taken into careful consideration by the intelligent teacher. Truth is similar to good food, in one respect at least; it must be taken in proper doses and in palatable form if it is properly to nourish the individual. I am told that babies, for example, are not to be fed chunks of *filet mignon.* Similarly, in teaching the young about human sexuality, great care must be taken to present the matter in a degree and in a form proportional to the capacity of the recipients.

It has never ceased to amaze me that this generation which boasts of having made such great strides in understanding human psychology, does not seem to understand what our great-grandparents instinctively knew, namely, that anything touching human reproduction is extremely stimulating for the young. Consequently, to respect the human body, the sanctuary of the Holy Spirit Who lives in men and women and in boys and girls sanctified by divine grace, great care must be taken to suit the presentation of biological, social and theological information about human reproduction to the emotional, intellectual and physiological condition of the catechized. Reverence for man, respect for the holiness of truth, regard for the instinctive, protective modesty of the young will dictate the teacher's approach.

After all, truth will make us free (Jn. 8:32). If a truth conveyed leads man to become a slave of his passions, there is nothing wrong with the truth, but with the manner in which it was presented. A teacher is not a movie camera or computer projecting what has been put into him or her. The teacher is a thinking person equipped to communicate a message in the manner best adapted to the students. It is an indication of the enormous confidence God Himself has in men and women that He has entrusted to us the vital and delicate task of communicating to mankind His truths of various kinds, rather than revealing them directly to each individual. We must respect that confidence by our honesty in teaching.

The Third Mark of Truth

The truth is catholic, that is, universal. It does not depend on geography, politics or race, or even history. Sometimes we are inclined to think that truth changes with the passage of years. The atom, for example, used to be the smallest particle of matter. Then someone came along and split it, so it no longer is. Is not this scientific proof that truths change? Of course not. It is not truth that changed, it is man who erred in the first instance. Man *thought* the atom to be the smallest particle, but, in truth, it wasn't. Many things we call "scientific truth" are only theories. For example, some scientists say that I evolved from tropical fish. I consider *that* a theory rather than a truth, because, for one thing, they are prettier.

Similarly, in the field of Catholic doctrine we must be precise in the use of the very word "truth." Christian *truth* never changes, but everything churchmen teach is not unchangeable truth. What Christ taught, what has been divinely revealed *is* the truth and is just as much true in Paris as it is in Peoria. We often call the sum total of this the deposit of the faith. Even the Magisterium of the Church cannot change what God has taught. That is one reason why marriage will remain indissoluble, because Jesus' proclaimed it so. The Church cannot change that.

But in the field of worship, in the organization of various religious activities, in works of penance, holy days and so forth, there is often room for changes according to local circumstances and the needs of a particular time in history. In these areas, there is room for legitimate argument over the propriety, the need, the efficacy of making adaptations. That is what Vatican Council II was all about; that is, it was a pastoral Council of the Church intended to bring methods, emphases, and approaches in the apostolate up to date to meet the needs of the times. None of the updating touched the deposit of the faith. You used to say *Credo in unum Deum.* Now you say: *I believe in one God.* The tongue is different, but the truth remains the same. The priest used to face the back wall of the church at Mass.

Now he faces the people. But the ministerial priesthood is still the same and not to be confused with the priesthood of the faithful.

Recent innovations in the Church have confused some people unnecessarily. Many times the reasons behind the changes were not explained clearly and seldom was the distinction between the substance and the accidents of the faith made clear to the faithful. Of course, there have not been lacking those who were unwilling to stop at prescribed changes and went on to institute substantial changes on their own initiative, for example, offering the Eucharist to those who do not believe that Christ is truly present in that sacrament. But such exaggerations do not invalidate the legitimate need for periodic improvements in the pastoral life of the Church.

Truth Is Apostolic

The fourth mark of the Church's truth is its apostolicity. This means that the deposit of faith, as distinguished from merely disciplinary and organizational norms, must be traceable back to Apostolic times. The Church teaches that all that is necessary for salvation is to be found in the Scriptures and Tradition ending in Apostolic times,[7] or, as a convenient date, at the death of the last surviving Apostle, St. John the Evangelist. The apostolicity of Catholic truth is an extremely useful measure of orthodoxy, because any teaching that contradicts what the Apostles taught is automatically to be rejected. As we saw above, truth is one. Since the Apostolic truth is sure, anything contrary to it is to be excluded from our doctrine.

Everything the Apostles taught could not have been totally clear even to them for they, too, lived by faith as do all just men (Rom. 1:17). They passed on to the

Church and to us what they had learned from Christ, Who, in turn, had been sent by His Father. Through the centuries there has taken place a gradual unfolding of Christ's original teaching.[8] Cardinal John Henry Newman called it "The Development of Doctrine." And Catholic doctrine is still developing, as we would expect, because the Eternal Truth is bottomless and provides endless food for human contemplation. However, development is not new revelation; development is not a change in the essential meaning of the word. Development is a flowering, a growth in implication, in understanding, in application always faithful to the original Word. To test, then, the purity of a given doctrine, it must be traceable back to Apostolic teaching. We do not say traceable back to the Scriptures themselves, because there are "many things Jesus did and taught which are not written in this book" (Jn. 21:25). It is not, however, the right of the individual Christian authoritatively to interpret Apostolic teaching for, "the task of giving an authentic interpretation of the Word of God, whether in its written form or in the form of tradition, has been entrusted to the living teaching office of the Church alone."[9]

Conscience

At this point one might ask where one's own conscience comes into play in all this. We are told we must follow our conscience. But if our conscience tells us to do one thing and the Church another, which are we to choose?

Here we must make a distinction between fact and good will. If a motorist is stopped by a policeman for going through a red light, he might say in all honesty: "I did not see it." The motorist may be as innocent as a lamb before God, but the fact is that he broke the law.

Somewhat the same situation exists in the moral law. Just as a motorist has the obligation to look for traffic lights, so men and women have the obligation to look for the norms of conduct which the Church teaches. Everyone has the obligation to form, to educate his or her conscience in a Christian manner. If one finds that he or she does not agree with the Church on a given point and deliberately acts contrary to the Church's teaching, that is something that will have to be taken up at the Last Judgment. When the Divine Judge asks: "Did you know the Church taught such and such?", will one have the courage to reply: "Yes, I did, Lord, but I did not agree." On the other hand, if one breaks God's law through honest error, there is no guilt involved.

Conclusion

My dear Brothers and Sisters in the Lord, you and I have the obligation as catechists to teach the truth to the young and to all those who come to us for advice and guidance in their struggle to reach eternal life. We are not sent by the Church to preach ourselves or our own opinions but "Jesus Christ and him crucified" (1 Cor. 2:2). We have the obligation to help our catechumens build firm foundations on which to construct their spiritual lives. Good foundations are not built with cracked bricks, watered-down mortar and crooked guidelines. Teach the solid truth; teach the whole truth; teach nothing but the truth, undiluted with things which men and women with "itching ears" like to hear (2 Tm. 4:3). For the Word of God is Truth Himself and the young who come to you have a right bought by the Blood of Christ to know Him as He wants to be known, as "a light that shines in the dark, a light that darkness could not overpower" (Jn. 1:15).[10]

NOTES

1. Pope John Paul II, Apostolic Exhortation *Catechesi tradendae*, no. 19 (October 16, 1979).

2. "A Catechism of Christian Doctrine," Revised edition of the Baltimore Catechism No. 2 (St. Anthony Guild Press, Paterson, N.J., 1962), p. 29.

3. Roman Breviary, Antiphon for Lent.

4. Pope John Paul II, Talk to the Faculty of the Catholic University of America, Washington, D.C., October 10, 1979.

5. Pope John Paul II, *Catechesi tradendae*, no. 61; 1 Tm. 6:22ff.

6. Pope John Paul I, Talk on the occasion of the *ad limina* visit of Philippine Bishops to the Holy See, September 28, 1979.

7. Vatican Council II, Dogmatic Constitution *Dei Verbum*, nos. 4 and 8.

8. *Ibidem*, nos. 8 and 24.

9. *Ibidem*, no. 10.

10. This talk, *The Right of the Catechized to the Truth*, is available on cassette from St. Paul Editions.

The Truth and "Pluralism"

Silvio Cardinal Oddi

This morning I took up briefly the subject of "Theological Pluralism." I would like to explore it a bit further this afternoon, with your help and the help of my fellow members on this panel.

A priest who works with me in Rome recounted the following story to me recently. He offers Sunday Mass and preaches his homily every week in the same Roman parish church. He noticed a young man in his early thirties assisting regularly at Mass and the Sacraments, and was impressed by his fidelity and devotion. One Sunday after Mass the young man politely inquired if he could ask the priest a question about the homily just delivered. The priest, of course, said, "Yes, by all means." The man explained his problem. He said: "You spoke today about the Eucharist and Transubstantiation, the Real Presence and the Paschal Sacrifice. I found it really interesting, but I have a little problem. At Communion time you open the tabernacle and take the Blessed Sacrament out to distribute to the people. Father, my problem is this: How does the Blessed Sacrament get into the tabernacle in the first place?"

Now, what does pluralism have to do with this man's problem? I think it has a lot to do with it and I think a catechetical discussion like this is the right place to bring the problem up. How much time are we able to give the average adult for his religious instruction? Or, how much time is the average child willing to give us to listen to religious instruction? For the average Catholic the Sunday sermon is virtually the only catechetical instruction he receives over the whole gamut of his life. He may make a retreat, or attend Bible discussions for a year or two, he may take a brief course when he marries or when his children are to be baptized. But is it not true that apart from Catholic school students, most Catholics receive very little religious instruction over a lifetime? If this is true, then do we have the time to teach the faithful about points in theology, concerning which a variety of opinions may be held? Should we not spend every available minute on the fundamentals of our Faith? And indeed *not omitting* the very practical points? For example, how the Blessed Sacrament gets into the tabernacle?

I would like to join in a good discussion on this point, and I feel safe, because I am surrounded by experts who will assist me if I am maneuvered into a corner.

What do you think "pluralism" is? Is it a good thing? Do we have time for it? Under what circumstances? Do we answer a child's question about the obligation of Sunday Mass by saying: "There are opinions, there are two opinions on that"? Do we suggest reading Hans Küng when teaching the infallibility of the Pope to the average Catholic?

Perhaps we could begin such a discussion by asking someone to volunteer a definition of pluralism, both theological and catechetical. I have little doubt that more than one definition would be proposed. And we must keep in mind that we are speaking as authentic teachers of the One, Holy, Roman Apostolic Church (we are discussing pluralism with regard to faith and morals as taught by our

Church) and not as professors in a course of the history of comparative religion.

How much pluralistic leeway can we legitimately permit? How profitable will such discussions be for the salvation of our charges? What are the advantages and the risk in devoting catechetical or sermon time to pluralism? Who will be humble enough to ask us the first question or to attempt a definition of pluralism in the sense I have just mentioned?

Introduction to the Panel

A special feature of the Cardinal Oddi Catechetical Day was the panel of specialists who represented sections of the People of God, groups of members of the Catholic Church in America.

Cardinal Oddi earlier had guided the initial planning of the panel in its design to reflect upon and to apply his keynote address on "The Right of the Catechized to the Truth."

On the day itself, Cardinal Oddi introduced the discussion.

He was succeeded on the panel by Mother M. Claudia, I.H.M., representing the Religious Sisters, who always have distinguished the Catholic Church in America by teaching the truth of the Catholic Faith to the children. Mother Claudia presented most positively the role of memory in childhood as the God-given power which preserves the right to this truth abidingly throughout life.

Mrs. Evelyn B. Vitz, wife of the leading psychologist, Dr. Paul C. Vitz, a mother and herself likewise a professor at New York University, represented Catholic parents, so deeply concerned that this "right of the catechized to the truth" not suffer any violation when it is the little children who are concerned.

Most Reverend Thomas J. Welsh spoke for the men of Holy Orders, to whom the Deposit of Faith has been entrusted in a special way by Jesus Himself when He taught and trained His Apostles.

Finally, the new generation, the promising young people whom God is raising up in the contemporary Church, were represented by Andrew J. Zwerneman, a lay catechist trained at a Pontifical Catechetical Institute and a member of the People Praise community in South Bend, Indiana. Cardinal John Wright always foresaw the emergence of these competent pastoral catechists. These new young people have a keen sense for the truth of the Catholic Faith and want it taught in the way of Pope John Paul II: whole and entire, without ambiguity.

These clear commentaries upon Cardinal Oddi's theme are presented with special thanks to each of the panelists.

Msgr. Eugene Kevane

The Call of Catholic Parents for Organic and Systematic Catechetical Teaching

Evelyn B. Vitz

I am speaking today primarily as a parent—and especially as a mother—about the important issues which are the subject of this conference. What I would like to articulate is the call of Catholic parents for organic and systematic Christian instruction.

What we are asking is that our children in the Catholic schools and CCD programs should be instructed in the basic teachings of the Church: the basic doctrines, prayers, devotions of the Faith—and taught to express this Faith in how they live. We are asking that the catechist should not feel free to discard elements of the Creed, for example, if they are, as it were, out of fashion, or if he or she doesn't agree with them: this we certainly ask. All of this is, I imagine, clear to everyone here today. This point has always been important; there have always been heresies. It is just more important today than it has been for a long time. One of the reasons why it is more important today is that the kind of catechesis that used to go on in the home, the Catholic home, is simply not reliably going on today. For one thing, there are so many mothers working outside of the home. They do not have the time and energy to give the kind of instruction in the Faith that Catholic mothers used to give. Moreover, many parents whose children are in Catholic schools are not themselves practicing Catholics. Many are nonpracticing; others are Protestants; and many are agnostics benevolently inclined toward but essentially ignorant of the teachings of Catholicism. (For example, when we first sent our eldest child to a Catholic school, we were not Catholics.) Obviously, such children will not be catechized at home.

Further, the catechesis that they do receive in school will go home with them to their parents. If it is sturdy and substantial, it will be able to catechize, indirectly, the parents as well. In a word, it is a whole family that you catechize. I think we should never underestimate what a powerful impact on parents the faith and devotion of their children can have. A couple of years ago, when I was already a Catholic, but a recent convert, my spiritual director told me I should start saying the Rosary. I didn't want to; I had great resistance to it. But I said I'd try. I decided to try saying it at home, though I was sure that our children—there were four of them, aged two to nine—would interrupt constantly and make it impossible. Maybe that's what I was hoping.... I started saying it in the evening after supper. By the second day, two of my children were already saying it with me, and soon the other two joined as well. They insisted upon saying it every night. They wouldn't go to bed without it. And my otherwise quite fierce four-year-old son said to me one day, after we'd been saying the Rosary for some months: "No matter where I am or what I am doing, I am always saying the Rosary in my heart." Now this is the sort of thing that just bowls over parents—especially recent converts and non-Catholics. The Spirit obviously moves so powerfully in children; who can deny it? But the question is: how many children in this country are really being exposed to the full power and range of the Catholic Faith today? How many are being taught to be informed and prayerful Catholics?

The answer is, of course: far too few. Many American Catholic schools and CCD programs are sadly deficient. The texts are weak, lopsided, askew—where they are not actually heterodox. One rather wishes that Nader's Raiders would go after some so-called "Catholic" schools: has a product ever been more mislabeled? Truth in advertising should surely require schools to describe what they really teach—and not just what they want parents and alumni to think they teach....

I am sure that you are better informed on the failings and errors of the catechetical texts than I am, as a parent. Where I am most aware of the deficiencies is in the preparation that the children receive for the sacraments. It is now commonplace for the Sacrament of Penance—reconciliation—to be delayed for several years after First Communion. And as to the preparation for First Communion, if our experience can serve as an example, it is simply not to be believed! When our eldest was attending special classes before First Communion, my husband attended every single class. (This was before we were Catholics.) In the fourteen sessions, more attention was paid to the United Nations than to the Mass. The elements were mentioned only in the last session or so. In fourteen sessions, the word "Catholic" never occurred. It was never explained why Christ died. Nor was the Mass ever described as a sacrifice. The Real Presence was never mentioned. (Our second child we had prepared for the sacraments privately—but how many parents have such resources?) What is interesting is that the parents only know what is going on—what is being taught in this sort of class—if they attend themselves. There is often no catechetical text being followed. You have to monitor this in person.

I can make one other comment on the flaky religion texts that I see: they look so boring. Religion is taught as something with no substance, no challenge. It is all too often a gut subject. As Father William Smith would put it, it's all "caring and sharing as intransitive verbs." Which means that the children, the smart children, are taught indirectly to think that religion is "dumb"—a contemptible subject—not worth their best efforts of mind or will.

Finally, let me speak briefly to what happens to children, Catholic children in particular, who don't receive a solid grounding in the Faith—and here I am speaking from a double vantage point: that of a mother and that of a college teacher. I teach at a large secular university. Now this past spring, I managed to offer a course on "The Saints." This topic drew an enrollment of over fifty students, to the amazement of my colleagues and the dean. The students came from extremely diverse backgrounds: there were practicing and nonpracticing Catholics, Protestants, a Unitarian, Jews, and Indian Jain, agnostics and atheists. The first day of class I had the students fill out a piece of paper with some information for me: name, major, other relevant courses, why they took this course, and their religious background. Let me share—as we say—some of the comments that the students raised as Catholics made about their religious background. A handful of them, a tiny handful, had had excellent religious instruction—but that was the exception. Even most of the devout students were—and knew they were—very poorly informed on their Faith. One girl wrote, tellingly: "My family is Catholic; I attended Catholic grade school, but my factual religious knowledge is lacking, due to the 'new' way of teaching religion—it's all experience, no facts." Many others wrote something on the order of "Catholic—but barely anything remembered from catechism," or "religious instruction, but didn't learn much." Several—art history majors—said that they were Catholic, but that everything they knew about Catholic teaching they had learned in art history classes.

Now students catechized as these students clearly had been are enormously vulnerable; they are under massive pressure, every day, to conform to the ideology and mores of secular society. Let me describe what university life is like today. These kids live in coed dorms, with contraception and abortion available—often free—at the university health service. Many of their college professors are ignorant of but also hostile toward and contemptuous of Christianity, and Catholicism in particular. These college students are taught, often directly, more often by innuendo, that it is not intellectually respectable to be a Christian. This idea is of course reenforced by the media, with whose biases we are all too familiar. What is there to help these young people? The Newman Club? Well, many a Newman Center has long since caved in both on doctrine and on practice, especially with regard to sexuality. At our Center, the holy water fonts stand permanently empty, and look like ash trays at the entrance to the church. In a word, the pressures on these kids to lapse from the Faith are enormous. Only those young people who have been powerfully vaccinated by a strong dose of Catholic teaching can resist the infection. They need more, a lot more, than to be taught about "feelings"; they need more than caring and sharing as intransitive verbs. They need a catechetical teaching that has muscle and brains—and that stimulates participation in the sacraments, and the expression of Christian love in daily life. And they need to receive this catechesis in the Catholic school setting. Without such teaching, with anything less, we can just write off hundreds of thousands of sloppily, sentimentally, vapidly educated young Catholics.

So as a mother, whose children are still a number of years from college—but time passes fast!—I hope and pray and plead that in their schools they may receive the kind of Christian instruction they need: one which will not only form their minds and hearts and consciences, but also serve as an armor against the many and great challenges to their Faith that they will meet in the years ahead.

But this instruction that we mothers hope and plead for is also something to which we—our children, rather—have a right; a God-given right as Christians, and a specific right, as Catholics, under Canon Law. There has been, as most of you know, a good deal of anguish recently over the "plight of the papist priest." Well, we papist parents—despite our concern and our frustration—are in some ways in an easier situation, and one that we should take advantage of. No bishop can transfer us to some other diocese. They can't send us off to Stony Lonesome or Pumpkin Patch. We stick around! We have to learn to be effective, persuasive, persistent reminders to those responsible for catechesis within our dioceses. We must state and restate what we expect, what we have a *right* to expect, by way of catechesis for our children. And if we get no satisfaction, we have to learn to document our grievances properly, and take them to Rome. We need a little bit of parental solidarity! In our struggles with the flaky catechists, we might do well to model ourselves on the widow who finally wore down the unjust judge. We must be patient, but persistent; ever charitable, but relentless in our pursuit of sound Christian catechesis.

The Place and Role of Memory as a God-given Natural Power, Especially Significant in the Formative Years of Childhood

Mother M. Claudia, I.H.M.

Working directly with our elementary school children, once a week in grades one through eight, has been one of the richest and most rewarding experiences of my life. God had some very delightful surprises waiting for me here in Arlington, and the story from St. Mark 10:13-16 became wonderfully alive for me. I would like to begin my simple contribution with it:

> "People were bringing little children to him, for him to touch them. The disciples turned them away, but when Jesus saw this, he was indignant and said to them, 'Let the little children come to me; do not stop them; for it is to such as these that the kingdom of God belongs. I tell you solemnly, anyone who does not welcome the kingdom of God like a little child, will never enter it.' Then he put his arms around them, laid his hands on them, and gave them his blessing."

What an indelible memory this experience must have been in the minds of those children and in the minds of the eager mothers who wanted them to touch Jesus personally! This thought is often in my own mind as I look at the youngsters before me, brought to us by their parents, eager for their children to touch Jesus through the religious instructions given and the inspiration to live what they are learning.

Perhaps instead of a strictly formal talk for these few minutes, we could all enter into a reflection on Jesus' words and on His attitude, born as it was of His own Jewish background as a child, learning from Mary and Joseph, His own boyhood lessons, the word of God. Surely He knew the Scriptures very well; He used them frequently. He must have turned each evening at the sunset with Mary and Joseph to recite the Shema: "Hear, O Israel! The Lord is your God, the Lord alone! Therefore, you shall love the Lord, your God, with all your heart and with all your soul, and with all your strength. Take to heart these words which I enjoin on you today. Drill them into your children. Speak of them at home and abroad, whether you are busy or at rest. Bind them at your wrist as a sign, and let them be as a pendant on your forehead. Write them on the doorposts of your houses and on your gates" (Dt. 6:4-9). God, His Father, wanted things learned and memorized, and wanted them spoken of again and again. Jesus, a little Boy, like our little children, learned and memorized many parts of the Old Testament. He knew the psalms by heart, for surely Mary and Joseph took most seriously, as they took all God's commands to them, the words: "Drill them into your children." In our meditation today, we can see the holy, gentle parents, quietly, reverently, teaching this remarkable young Son what they had been told to teach Him.

Jesus memorized these lessons for He used them spontaneously. This fact, together with Pope John Paul's words from *Catechesi Tradendae* on knowing by memory the truths of our Faith, helps us to understand better the value of using the memory in our work with the children, and teaching them to know and respect the great power of recall it allows. These are Pope John Paul's words:

> "At a time when, in nonreligious teaching in certain countries, more and more complaints are being made about the unfortunate consequences of disregarding the human faculty of memory, should we not attempt to put this faculty back into use in an intelligent and *even an original way* in catechesis, all the more since the celebration or memorial of the great events of salvation history requires a precise knowledge of them?"

The Holy Father then continues with a list of key truths that should be learned by heart: certain prayers, formulas, definitions, doctrinal points that far from becoming parroted memorization, can and should become the force for initial learning about God and His Church. In the preparation for the Bishops' Synod on *Catechetics in Our Time,* the assembled shepherds of the world acknowledged that especially among children and young people is there a growing need for a more knowledgeable and consistent faith. Both Pope Paul VI and Pope John Paul II have followed up this expressed need by encouraging every possible interest and effort with our children of today, who will be the Church of tomorrow. The knowledge and strength we give them now by introducing memorization into the learning of religion during these formative years will be the source of hopeful confidence for a lifetime. With expanded concentric repetition as the children grow in wisdom, age, and grace, these memorized treasures can become the rock on which they can build a firm foundation. With careful introduction and an enthusiasm born of faith in himself and God's grace, the catechist can teach the students to reflect on what is being learned. The children should be given a clear explanation of what we mean by memorizing with understanding. They can be taught that some things, indeed many things, can be learned by their own reasoning powers, if they master the art of thinking, and that other things are mysteries that no man can explain fully, no matter how learned he becomes. Only God Himself knows these things, but He gives us the gift of faith to believe and accept them, and this faith is one of His greatest gifts to His children. Presenting even profound ideas to the children in a way that shows our great reverence for their God-given ability to absorb them can start the children off to a marvelous exploration of what the Church is, what she stands for, what she teaches as doctrine, and what she demands of her faithful members! The Holy Father mentions especially in his list for memorization certain words of Jesus, and the basic formal prayers of the Church. What a beautiful task the teacher has: to introduce these to the young people being catechized—thus fulfilling their right to the truth! From the very beginning, the students must be brought to know that we reach God by two special means: one, learning about Him through earnest study; and two, using what we learn to help us love Him more and to develop a prayer-relationship with Him, so that what we learn becomes part of our life here and now. Our faith is not merely a lesson learned, but a life lived! The youngsters can be taught that they are living books of faith, walking about among the people, "bringing Jesus' good news to everyone they meet."

It has been my delightful privilege to experiment with the Holy Father's suggestion of restoring *memory* to its rightful place in the field of catechetics, and of providing the material to be memorized. In both school and CCD classes, as well as with individual children the Lord sent to me to prepare for the sacraments, I have pursued this suggestion. There is not sufficient time to talk about methods or textbooks today, both of which need a great deal of thought and evaluation. However in my own efforts, I presented doctrine, or prayer, or an important point of faith; explained it; used the blackboard; allowed time for the students to think about it with their own great gifts from God of intellect, free will and memory, and these I mentioned over and over so that they would come to understand and appreciate God's gifts to His human beings; gave them time for memorizing some brief, clear definition to summarize, and then closed with a prayer that the Holy Spirit would help us all to remember what we had learned and put it into immediate practice that very day.

For me, the results of this experiment have been amazing and gratifying. The children love learning doctrine, have come to understand what it is, and why it is important, and they are proud and happy to memorize the truths of their Faith as taught by the Church. Convinced of the power of the Creed and the Our Father and knowing the importance they have for the full knowledge and practice of our Faith, I stressed through the first, the transmission of faith-content, and through the second, the grace of prayer needed to transmit Jesus to all.

"There is nothing new under the sun!"—a text that has always intrigued me and which I applied, by using an old, and I believe quite forgotten tool: *The Religion Clock*—as a means to help the children place and memorize points of doctrine. The children find this a fascinating way to learn and to remember the great truths of their Faith, and a real challenge to know it by heart. The thought came to me as I began to note how constantly numbers are used today in every field, economic, academic, professional, and how significant they have come to be in communication, for telephones, addresses, zip codes, etc. And so I told the children that numbers should and could be used as a great help to them in memorizing their religious truths, recalling how often and what a large part numbers play in Scripture. Even our little first-graders love this unique way. They feel as if they know Pope John Paul personally—they've heard so much about him—and they know he wants them to memorize because I have used this as a strong motivating point. Sometimes the little ones say: "Would Pope John Paul be proud of us?" And I know he would be.

The Religion Clock is a large-sized cardboard clock, with a cross in the middle to let us know it isn't just an ordinary clock. Each number recalls some important point of dogma or doctrine. The children have learned many truths by using it. At times, they have added their own points to the numbers and this makes me happy because I know they are thinking.

No wonder Jesus loved the little children and told us to be like them. Their minds are open, loving, and ready to receive His truth, His way, and indeed His life. I am astounded at what they can grasp: they can be taught what *grace* is—surely an important but neglected concept in our day; they can learn to recognize in their minds God's great gifts of intellect, free will, and memory. They can be prodded to think out why free will is a beautiful but dangerous gift. They can memorize the entire message of doctrine contained in the Religion Clock, and they can stop at any number to explain. No words are too big for them to learn. No ideas too profound to present prayerfully to their receptive young souls. They need definitions for they do not have a vocabulary for abstract things, and the words of definitions are blessed building blocks for later meditation and understanding.

We must never allow ourselves to be discouraged or impatient with results that we see. Often the greatest results are preserved in hidden seeds planted in hearts by a dedicated, fearless bearer of the truth. Pope John Paul told priests in Rome recently that the majority of Christians today feel bewildered, confused, perplexed and even misled by the widely disseminated ideas that contradict revealed truth. We know he is right. His solution to such a widespread disheartening condition was not to give up—he is not that kind of a shepherd!—but, and these are his words for those priests and for us: "It is necessary today to be patient, and to begin all over again from the very beginning of faith."

That is what it means to be an apostle of truth in 1983. With our children we must seize this special time in their lives to bring them to Jesus and His Church by every means available. And we must remember that we have thousands of solid, practicing Catholics in our country today who memorized definitions and prayers and formulas, not without explanation, either, as some would claim, but by patient teachers of religion who were not always blessed with theology courses and degrees, but who had a strong, unshakable faith and good common sense that helped them to teach, to encourage, and to inspire another generation to know, love and serve God in this world, and to be happy with Him forever in the next.

The Bishop and the Handing On of the Faith

Bishop Thomas J. Welsh

"Through the ministry of the bishop, Christ Himself continues to proclaim the Gospel and to confer the mysteries of faith on those who believe" (homily, Mass for the ordination of a bishop).

What a joy to be part of this day of grace in this special Holy Year of 1983! Redemption of mankind is surely *the* Good News of all our efforts at catechesis. It is Providence, not coincidence, that this year of 1983 was ushered in by Cardinal Ratzinger's talk in Paris and Lyons, and that Cardinal Oddi himself is with us today. What a link we have with Christ's teaching Church: the vicar of the Vicar of Christ guiding our day. Who knows what the rest of such a year may bring us from the Lord?

While I prepared my paper in advance I was confident that this day had to be one in which we stress fundamentals (those four stressed by Cardinal Ratzinger in January: Apostles' Creed, Sacraments, Ten Commandments and Our Father) and in which we stress the nature of the Church.

My part in this panel highlighting fundamental aspects of catechetics is twofold: 1) to reflect on the catechetical apostolate from the vantage point of the Church/bishop/Magisterium, and 2) to conclude on a note of reminder that it is only by the handing on of the Creed that we can fulfill our obligation of bringing children from the grace of Baptism to Catholic adult life.

On the first point, noting that Cardinal Ratzinger mentioned his own "horror story" example (a lady told him that her son was learning the "sayings of the Lord" but not the Sacraments and the Creed) and noting the concern already expressed today, I encourage you to reflect on these stories and your own perhaps. They offer us several clues for our positive response: The Church is not described as *the authentic* teacher of Christ's truth; membership in the Church is not offered as valuable because of the grace that its Sacraments give.

I suggest that the Lord is offering us the help we need (and offering today's young people that grace they need) in the persons of our Holy Father John Paul II and his Predecessors in this century. Cardinal Baum, shortly after the death of Pope Paul, told me that he promised himself to refer to him always as the *great* Pope Paul. He *was* great. Think of *Humanae Vitae* as a prophetic document predicting the increasing evils of contraception and abortion but also ushering in the great advances in Natural Family Planning. Think of the larger topic of Evangelization, as it were Pope Paul's last will and testament. Let me offer some further examples of that style of catechetics (calling him always the *great* Pope Paul): when we come to John XXIII we mention *Pacem in Terris* at once; we should also mention his daily rosary. When we show a picture of the lovely smile of John Paul I, we should mention how pro-life he was (e.g., comparing the Holy Innocents slain by the soldiers with babies today slain by their own mothers). In this very topic of catechetics mention that *Catechesi Tradendae* was the work of three Popes, that John Paul II sees himself as Successor to John and Paul and, of course, to Peter!

God is giving us such tremendous leaders; we ought to tremble for not using them more. John Paul in Poland (you can name your country)! We ought to quote him, cite his authorship of this document and his insistence on fundamentals. His call for purity, for confession, for vocations. His being the Successor to Saint Peter, kissing children, scolding the priest in Central America and the sister in Detroit, meeting this year with United States bishops in Rome. We ought to explain the *ad limina* visit idea.

Perhaps listening to and quoting him may alert us all that we do have the truth.

It is in the new Code and beautifully put in Canon 773 and other canons. "There is a proper and serious duty, *especially on the part of pastors of souls,* to provide for the catechesis of the Christian people so that the faith of the faithful becomes a living, developing, and productive faith through formation in doctrine and through the experience of Christian living."

It is in *Lumen Gentium* (no. 25): "Among the most important duties of bishops, that of preaching the Gospel has pride of place. For the bishops are heralds of the faith, who draw new disciples to Christ; they are authentic teachers, that is, teachers endowed with the authority of Christ, who preach the faith to the people assigned to them, the faith which is destined to inform their thinking and direct their conduct; and under the light of the Holy Spirit they make that faith shine forth...."

It is, as I quoted at the beginning, in the bishop's ordination ceremony. He is asked, for example: "Are you resolved to maintain the Deposit of Faith, entire and uncorrupt, as handed down by the Apostles and professed by the Church everywhere and at all times?"

It does not take much reflection to perceive that these charges and challenges made to the bishop are shared in by all who assist him in catechesis. Not even angels can teach another Gospel, Saint Paul reminded the Galatians

(Gal. 1:8). Our Lord's way of putting it is that it were better for a man to be drowned than that he lead children astray (Mt. 18:6).

The devil is alive and well. He is the father of lies, and I believe we have seen him working with a lot of success in catechetics (present company excepted, of course). But it was our present Holy Father whose retreat for the great Pope Paul and his staff was entitled "A Sign of Contradiction"!

Popes Paul and John Paul—surely living examples of a radical conversion to Christ and both men examples of love and concern for children. (We take this for granted now in John Paul but I cherish the memory of a general audience of Pope Paul near the end of his life and his smiling and laughing exchange with a youth group from Lyons.)

These Popes lead us. John Paul seems to have published the *Catechesi Tradendae* in order to insist that the Faith be taught at all levels in its integrity. Saint John did not say God is complex. He did say God is love, and loving Popes believe children can love too, can love the Redeeming God. We had experiences several years ago of people deciding that children could not make First Penance before First Communion. On this catechetical day we ought to include a prayer for the late Cardinal Wright! Remember his statement: "The hand in the cookie jar today—uncorrected—is the hand in the city treasury tomorrow." Remember the consequences too—young people not wanting to be confirmed because they had never made First Penance. How many have strayed because of that!

This Pope who loves children also has that big M on his coat of arms. While he was allowed to suffer the attempt on his life, he was spared to us on May 13 by Our Lady of Fatima. (If people question that statement, we can respond innocently that that is what *he* believes!) Providence thus directed us to Fatima and to three very young children. One making her First Communion at age six by exception because *she knew her catechism.* The other two still too young. Babies almost at the time of the Apparition, 10, 8, 7, yet being raised and trained by good parents and older sisters and brothers. Babies, almost, but visited by Our Lady and entrusted with a message for world peace *and* galvanized into personal holiness by a vision of hell. They were old enough to understand, to be strong, to be good, to do penance for sinners. Francesco and Jacinta are long since with the Lord and Our Lady in heaven. Lucy is still with us—a living relic as it were—like the waters of Lourdes. We have not really heeded "the Lady." We have not really followed the children's example of prayer and penance. Perhaps making them patrons of catechesis will open a door. Study Fatima with that thought and then go and teach. Fatima's lesson may well be the means to bring children from the grace of Baptism to Catholic adult life—and heaven.

The Importance of the Elements of Christian Doctrine

Andrew J. Zwerneman

The task before us today is both exciting and sobering at the same time. Our age, on the one hand, is an age of renewal, and despite the problems that face the Christian people today, many great things are happening among God's children.

Yet, we here today are keenly aware of the immensity of our task as catechists, teachers, parents, and pastors. Not only are there huge numbers of Christians who need sound catechesis, there are significant obstacles—intellectual and spiritual—that pose stiff opposition to the authentic presentation of Christian truth. Personally, I am encouraged by today's gathering. Firstly, it is heartening to know of others who are dedicated to the catechetical apostolate; and secondly, the intellectual and spiritual community fostered here today serves to strengthen both our resolve and ability to heed the truth of Christ and to teach it.

I've been asked to discuss a topic that cuts right to the heart of our present catechetical age: that is, the importance of stating the elements of Christian doctrine in religion textbooks, programs and syllabi, so as to distinguish the official teaching of the Church clearly from the explanation of that same teaching.

Education, and here I particularly mean catechesis, is an essential element in transmitting life from one generation to the next and is indeed one of the most important human activities. As catechists, we are called to hand on a living heritage to our children and students. As we catechize our brothers and sisters in the Lord, I believe it is helpful to be mindful of what their education is all about. Christian education involves fostering the development of the rational faculty of the students and the appropriation of Christian truth in their lives so that they might live as sons and daughters of God and disciples of Christ. In catechesis, we hope to develop our students' ability to perceive the truth and profess it faithfully, to help their minds embrace the truth of Christ, and their hearts Christian holiness.

Scripture teaches us that the Truth will set us free. This Truth is first and foremost the Truth of the Person of Jesus Christ Himself, given to us by the grace of God, handed down from the Apostles, and presented through the teaching of the Church exercising her ordinary and universal Magisterium. Christian doctrine, as presented by the Magisterium, is the touchstone and the anchor for catechists and authors of catechetical materials as we present the truth of Christ, the very Truth that will set us free.

In the *General Catechetical Directory,* it is explained that: "The greatest importance must be attached to catechisms published by ecclesiastical authority. Their purpose is to provide, under a form that is condensed and practical, the witnesses of Revelation and of Christian Tradition as well as the chief principles which ought to be useful for catechetical activity, that is for personal education in faith. The witnesses of Tradition should be held in due esteem, and very great care must be taken to avoid presenting as doctrines of the faith special interpretations which are only private opinions or the views of some theological school. The doctrine of the Church must be presented faithfully."[1]

Clearly, the Church is concerned that the distinction between doctrine and explanation or commentary not be or a schoolmate, or the child of a friend, our own child, or one of our CCD students. Here I have in mind the contemporary Catholic, particularly if he's young, whose religious education and personal religious convictions are weak and unstable. Surrounded, indeed undercut, by the skepticism, disbelief and doctrinal pluralism so prevalent in our time, he is, quite expectedly, confused.

It is this very kind of brother or sister in the Church who deserves to know exactly what the Church teaches. He shares with all men the desire to know the truth, particularly divine truth. But furthermore, as a member of the Catholic Church, his due is to receive at least the basic, essential teaching of his Church. As a Catholic student, he needs that basic ordered knowledge of God and His Revelation. Upon this knowledge the rest of his religious education can be built, and this doctrine will serve as the touchstone and anchor for all his questions, studies and pursuits as a student of the Faith.

More broadly, as a disciple of Christ, if he is to pursue the vision of greatness that each Christian is called to, that is, the constant vision of what with the grace of God is possible not only in this life but in the next as well, he needs that touchstone which is doctrine as he endeavors to explore the depths of the spiritual, moral, and intellectual life of the Church. The Christian needs something sure, something certain, an anchor as it were which holds steady his religious education. He needs that basic ordered knowledge, that touchstone to which he can return again and again, a core or foundation upon which his Christian pursuit for truth is built but which in itself is steady and permanent. Doctrine serves this purpose.

The Holy Father, Pope John Paul II, has voiced his concern about what he sees as unfaithfulness to Church doctrine. In *Catechesi Tradendae,* for example, he warns against catechetical materials that "deliberately or unconsciously omit elements essential to the Church's faith."[2] More recently, at the fifth session of the International Council for Catechesis this past spring, he commented that the "faith is sustained on reality, it lives on vital contents which are expressed in the various professions of faith. Catechesis, therefore, must have a vital bond with these contents."[3] Indeed, a teacher or student should be able to open a textbook or any kind of catechetical material and find those "vital contents" clearly stated and clearly distinct from explanation or commentary; those "vital contents" that sustain us in reality. If a catechumen fails to grasp the Truth of Christ, then he has, in a most devastating way, failed to grasp reality, or as the saying goes: "he's out of touch." We must ensure that our students not be out of touch but in full communion with the Redeemer of Man, the Lord whose saving Word brings light and freedom to human life.

It seems to me that modern man, especially the modern Christian, more than ever, needs an intellectual touchstone and anchor. The entire twentieth century, particularly with its fast-moving technological and scientific developments, is a broad testimony to man's need for basic ordered knowledge. It is certainly true that man cannot fully participate in contemporary society without adequate information and education. Schools and families across the country are scrambling to implement computer training in their children's education. No one wants their child or student to fall behind the times. Certainly, much of this thrust is needed. After all, people need information, knowledge and good education in order to succeed as intelligent human beings.

It seems to me that this principle holds true for Christians in a special way. Knowledge of the vital contents of Christian faith enables the individual Christian to take hold of the present age. More than ever, the People of God need the teaching of Christ, clear, distinct and in its entirety. It really is a wonderful and valuable gift for a catechist or the author of catechetical materials to give Christ's teaching—the doctrine of the Church—to his students, thereby opening the door to the Lord's saving truth. Modern man urgently needs the Church's apostolic witness, that truth which will set him free; that truth which will be his touchstone for his intellectual, spiritual and moral pursuits; and that truth which will enable him to be a strong, steadfast Christian in the modern world.

Finally, I'd like to encourage all of you as catechists, parents, and pastors to continue in your work. Take heart by this catechetical day and all that the Lord is doing in our age, and let us be joyful and confident as we engage in this most noble apostolate, serving Christ and His Truth at all times.

NOTES

1. *General Catechetical Directory*, no. 19.
2. *Catechesi Tradendae*, no. 49.
3. *L'Osservatore Romano*, May 30, 1983; English edition.

The Good Samaritan

Homily of Silvio Cardinal Oddi on the Fifteenth Sunday of the Year in the Cathedral of the Diocese of Arlington, July 9, 1983.

It is a great pleasure for me to be the recipient of your warm hospitality here in the Diocese of Arlington. You have shown yourself to be Good Samaritans, making a stranger feel at home. But to tell the truth, I do not feel a stranger because a sense of the unity of the Church takes possession of me as I go from place to place, from culture to culture, from language to language, for, in spite of superficial differences, we are one in baptism, one in faith and members of the same Mystical Body of Christ.

The Christian message of universal love toward others, regardless of where the others come from, what social rank they hold, how they dress or what they speak, has made an impact on the world that we often overlook. The Church has preached sexual equality, political freedom and equity in material things from the very beginning. Listen to St. Paul: "and there are no more distinctions between Jew and Greek, slave and free, male and female, but all of you are one in Christ Jesus" (Gal. 3:28-29).

This truth is, of course, at the heart of the drama of this morning's Gospel of the Good Samaritan, who is the symbol of the man and woman born in Jesus. The point of the story depends on the Samaritan's political and religious background. Genetically he was of the same race as the Jews, that is, of the man lying on the highway, the victim of robbers, and of the other travelers who passed by the wounded man, without stopping to help him. But because of historical reasons there were religious and political differences between Jews and Samaritans which made them enemies.

Nevertheless, the Samaritan helped the Jew, his enemy, even when others who had had much more reason to do so, did not. When you ponder this story, can you not see the faces of Jesus' audience, who were probably all Jews? They must have been very annoyed to have Jesus attribute more virtue to one who was not of the "Chosen People" than to the Chosen People themselves.

But, if Jesus would repeat the story to a group of us today, might not some of us be embarrassed, too? Do not we also often give a restricted definition to the word "neighbor," and are we not often more prone to help people who will be able to help us, rather than people who are simply unable to help themselves and whose contribution to our own welfare would probably be nil? Do we not tend to think of "neighbor" as the person next door of the same social class, of the same color, of the same language, who will lend us his lawnmower when ours breaks down?

In the Gospel of St. Luke, however, Jesus tells us that politics, religion, and culture have nothing to do with "neighbor," and even when one's own brothers ignore him, as did the priest and Levite, such neglect does not relieve us who have no relation to the needy man except our common humanity.

Missionary priests, brothers, sisters and lay people go to the far corners of the earth to preach the Gospel. They preach among other things the "new commandment": "That you love one another as I have loved you." But when people in those faraway countries look back to Christian countries, do they see in practice the wide interpretation of "neighbor" that Jesus exemplifies in today's Gospel? I think they do in some cases, but not in all.

Jesus' concept of neighbor is anyone who needs help, even if one can bring forth all sorts of reasons for not helping. Did Jesus wait until we sinful men and women became lovable before redeeming us? If He had, we never would have been redeemed. He loved us when we were still in our sins. He expects us to love others, even those with whom we have little or nothing in common. Why? Because He invites us to follow His example. Recall the simple, beautiful story of the little girl who was carrying a child almost bigger than she was. "Is he not heavy?" someone asked. "No, he is my brother."

"Have we not given enough?" "Will they appreciate what we do?" "What do we have in common?" "Should not his own kind help first?" The answer to all these questions is: "<u>He is my neighbor, and therefore I shall do what I can.</u>"

If Christian countries would expand their generosity to the needy, would bury cultural, political and racial differences, the job of the missionary would become easy, for the practice of neighborliness in the Christian sense is extremely attractive.

We can pick our neighborhood, but we cannot pick our neighbor. Every man, woman and child is our neighbor because, like us, he or she is a child of God. The Samaritan's selfless gesture toward the injured Jew did not mean that the Samaritan wished to embrace Judaism and reject his own religion, no more than our kindness to others means that we sympathize with their political aims or religious persuasion. Our sensitivity to the needs of others only means that we see the face of Jesus in the people of lands suffering drought, in civilians who suffer the violence of war, in prisoners of conscience, in those who suffer every kind of oppression. When we see Jesus in the miserable, we see rightly, for He became a man like us in all except sin.

If you read today's Gospel carefully, you will note that Jesus did not define the word neighbor. Rather, He created a living image of what a true neighbor is and called you and me to action, saying in the last line of the Gospel: "Go you and do likewise." Our faith is nourished by prayer, the sacraments, the liturgy, by good reading and study, but that is not the sum and substance of Catholicism. Our faith must be *lived*.

Living and Teaching Christ

Homily of Silvio Cardinal Oddi at a Mass of Graduation, Notre Dame Catechetical Institute, Middleburg, Virginia, July 10, 1983.

My dear Graduates, Sisters and Friends:

I have been invited here today to offer the Holy Sacrifice of the Mass and to present to the graduates, who have successfully finished the required studies, their catechetical Diploma, testifying to the certification of the Sacred Congregation for the Clergy and their own professors that they are qualified to go into the world to proclaim the message of Our Lord Jesus Christ. I have already congratulated you individually, and I now congratulate you all together.

The diploma you have received is no ordinary academic passport. It is unique because it attests that you have received approval for your work, both from His Excellency, the Most Rev. Bishop of Arlington, through his representatives here at Notre Dame Institute, and from the Office of the Holy See charged with the supervision of catechesis in all its aspects throughout the world. Successors of the Apostles certify, therefore, that in their judgment you are equipped to teach the doctrine of the Church, to mature the faith of the catechized, to form true disciples of Christ by steeping them in a deeper and more systematic knowledge of their beliefs as handed down to us from the Apostles themselves. You have been found worthy of this holy work. I salute you! I congratulate you!

Although the Gospel of this morning's Mass is the one that corresponds by liturgical norm to the Fifteenth Sunday of the Year in this present cycle of the Church's readings, it seems as if it were deliberately chosen to launch you into the catechetical world, for in it Jesus gives a superb example of the art of evangelizing, of teaching what His Father sent Him to teach, of what the Church sends us to teach.

Note how Our Lord immediately involves the lawyer personally in dialogue. Can't you visualize the same exchange between a student and a catechist?

Student: "How can I get to heaven?"

Catechist: "What does the Bible say; what does the Church say?"

Student: "I do love God. But how do I love my neighbor, and who is my neighbor?"

And so forth. It amuses me to read what some self-appointed experts have written about the question-and-answer method being no longer valid. It is not the only method, but it was a favorite method of Jesus Himself, and He used it tellingly.

By involving His questioner in a discussion, the lawyer is forced to think, and Jesus leads the discussion so that the point He wishes to make will emerge from it. Love of God and neighbor is the essence of the law.

But then Jesus suddenly switches from abstract theology to the concrete. He does not give a sociological definition of the word "neighbor." He tells a story, one of the greatest stories in all literature: graphic, clear, unforgettable. Jesus invites the lawyer to advance from a knowledge of the theory of Christianity to its practice. It is not enough to know how to define "neighbor." What is required is to *be* a neighbor. When Jesus ascertained that the lawyer had gotten the point, He said to him: "Go and do likewise."

My dear Sisters, the Church is sending you today through your superiors and through your respective bishops to teach Jesus Christ, in exactly the same manner in which the Church sent St. Paul to the Gentiles. Paul, on whose teachings millions of words have been written over the centuries, was not himself a theologian in the modern sense of the term. He was an apostle, an evangelizer sent to bring the Good News to all men. Jesus is the Good News, and Paul himself said that he went to "preach Christ crucified." This means that he sought to preach in such a way that his hearers would imitate Christ, not merely understand what Christ taught, but live as Christ lived and acted. Paul sought to teach what Jesus did and said so that his hearers would be identified with the mind and will of Jesus, so that they would "put on Jesus Christ."

Your catechetical mission will be counted a success when the world is able to see Christ in the young people you catechize. This is your goal, not an easy one by any means, but an inescapable one. When your catechumens show forth in their lives Jesus loving others, Jesus serving others, Jesus teaching others, Jesus sacrificing Himself for others, you will prove that your superiors had reason to approve you.

The first step toward this sublime goal is, of course, to become more Christ-like yourselves. But do not forget that many people in high places did not like Christ, and, if you become like Him, there are many who will not like you. The world loves its own. It does not love those who are a reproach to it. So if your purity of heart, your generosity, your fidelity to the Church and to the charism of your founders constitute a threat to those who live by the values of this world, be prepared to suffer.

In awarding you a catechetical Diploma this morning, the Church did not give you a free ticket to heaven. She has given you a challenge to serve, and to serve her Spouse, Who is also yours. The challenge is to live and to so teach that with St. Paul you will be able to say, "be followers of me, as I am also of Christ" (1 Cor. 4:16), and, in turn, you will be able to say to them: "Go now and do likewise."

Bring Light into Darkness

Homily of Silvio Cardinal Oddi at a Mass for the Daughters of St. Paul, Jamaica Plain, Boston, Massachusetts, July 11, 1983.

My dear Sisters:

It is, as you may have noticed, a particular joy for me to visit you. I have known the Daughters of St. Paul from their very foundation and knew Don Alberione and Mother Thecla many years ago. So it is a great comfort for me to see your work spread so far and wide even in my own lifetime, for the Hand of God is obviously upon you.

The Mass we are celebrating today is that of Saint Benedict, the patron of Europe. The saint carries that title with good reason because the monks he founded remained bulwarks of the faith when European civilization was collapsing around them due to the invasion of the Barbarians and the Migration of Nations across the face of Europe. Their monasteries became oases of learning and peace in a desert of ignorance and violence; their liturgies became beacons of belief in Jesus Christ in the Dark Ages which followed the invasion of hordes who had never heard of the Son of Mary; their rule established a rock of stability in a world that every day became more precarious.

I venture to say that, on a smaller scale, this little community of the Daughters of St. Paul has a role to play in the history of today's Church similar to the role of the followers of St. Benedict. I hope I do not offend your modesty if I repeat to you what one of the Auxiliary

Bishops of Boston told me last year. He said that the Sisters in this house are among the most dedicated he knows, and that there are more candidates for the Daughters of St. Paul than in all the other postulancies and novitiates of the Archdiocese combined.

I could not refrain from asking myself why. Why should the Daughters of St. Paul continue to grow, when so many other communities of Sisters are dying? I dare say there are many reasons, but I have observed two. First, you know who you are and, second, you wish to be known as who you are.

You are women of all ages and of many nationalities who have consecrated yourselves publicly to Jesus Christ or are in the process of doing so. You have taken, or will take, public vows of poverty, chastity and obedience. You believe that your public dedication to Christ and His Church will inspire others, and so you wish to wear a visible sign of that consecration, your habit. You do not serve the Church merely eight hours a day, but twenty-four, seven days a week, so you are always a Sister, not only during "working hours."

Perseverance in your calling is not easy today because you are surrounded by spiritual whirlpools seeking to suck you under the swirling waters. The Benedictine life in the Dark Ages was not easy either. There was physical danger from outside attack; some of Benedict's own followers tried to poison him, there were surely temptations from the Barbarian chiefs who must have offered the monks rewards of power and wealth if they would leave the monastery to share their knowledge and skills with earthly princes.

You, too, will be tempted to try to find a compromise between this world and the next. You will wonder if a dress seen on another "modern" religious would not look good on you. You might begin thinking that you could do more for your apostolate living alone in an apartment, rather than in a big convent. You might hear that you could get more done if you were to give less time to prayer, community or personal. Temptations against the true religious life are today many and subtle, but it is obvious by looking at you that the grace of God has defended you up until now.

Your humility has surely had a lot to do with your continued growth. You do not wish to be first with innovations. You are not trying to pull ahead of the Church, but with the Church, with the Holy Father and the Bishops whom God has sent to lead us. But this humility will not save you from persecution. A donkey is the most humble of animals, but when he sees what his rider does not see, he gets beaten.

One of my favorite Bible stories is that about Balaam's donkey in the Book of Numbers. Balaam was a type of medicine man, and he used to sell his services to curse or bless people according as he was hired. So the people of Moab hired Balaam to curse the Jews with whom they were at war. Balaam set out on his donkey to curse the Jews, but he had not traveled very far when the donkey refused to go any further. Balaam could not figure out why the donkey would not advance, but the donkey knew why—an Angel of God was standing in the middle of the road with a drawn sword in his hand. Balaam could not see the Angel and beat the donkey to move. The donkey figured it was better to take a beating than to be run through with the sword, so he refused to advance. Balaam beat him some more. Finally Balaam, too, was allowed to see the Angel, and he stopped beating the donkey only when the Angel had explained everything.

It is not infrequent in the Church that the most humble see the Angel: Bernadette of Lourdes, the Curé d'Ars,

Catherine of Siena and so many others. But instead of being listened to, they are beaten until the Lord opens people's eyes, often through sad experience.

I do not wish to discourage you, my dear Sisters, but to alert you. You are on the right path, but the right road is not necessarily the easy road. Do not be detoured from your goal of testifying to religious values by those who no longer understand in what the religious life consists. We should all try to be God's donkeys, that is, unwilling to move along a road which He has blocked. We should keep our eye on His Angel who is made known to us through our legitimate superiors, especially by our Bishop and the Holy Father.

In this morning's Gospel, Our Lord tells us that we are the branches of His vine. What good are we if we are cut off from Jesus? Can we bear fruit of ourselves, apart from Him? Remain, my dear Sisters, on the vine so that the Blood of Jesus may run through you and produce fruit, forty, sixty, a hundredfold.

The Holy Year and Reconciliation

Message of Silvio Cardinal Oddi to the Eternal Word Television Network, Birmingham, Alabama, July 15, 1983.

St. Peter's Square lies just below the window of my office in Rome. This year it is a moving sea of color as tens of thousands of pilgrims in their varied national dress pass leisurely through the square on their pious way to the Holy Door of St. Peter's Basilica. While the Holy Year indulgence can be gained in one's own country, many Catholics have wished to go to Rome itself to commemorate the Holy Year of the Redemption.

Our beloved Holy Father, Pope John Paul II, proclaimed this extraordinary Holy Year (extraordinary because usually it is celebrated only every twenty-five years) to recall the nineteen hundred and fiftieth anniversary of the traditional year of Christ's death and resurrection, 33 A.D., the year in which mankind was redeemed from sin and restored to grace.

As human beings we are a mixture of the material and the spiritual. God's pardon of our sins is a spiritual reality, but we like to do something physical, something visible to symbolize that forgiveness. The purpose of the Holy Year is to induce men and women to ask God's forgiveness for the wrongs they may have done. So the most vital part of the Holy Year observance is the inner conversion, the change of heart of the individual who asks God's pardon for the past and promises to do better in the future. Each man and woman who makes the Holy Year reenters, as it were, into the grace of God.

This is what the Holy Door symbolizes, and that is the reason for the pious custom of kissing it on passing through it. It is just an ordinary door of a church designated by the Bishop, but as one passes through it, one symbolically passes from the sinful world into God's house, from the darkness of sin into the light of grace.

This is why the heart of the Holy Year observance is the reception of the Sacrament of Penance, making one's confession to a priest who represents God and who forgives sins in God's name, carrying out what Jesus said to His Apostles in the Gospel of St. John: "Whose sins you shall forgive, they are forgiven them."

No one enjoys admitting one's faults to a priest. Our pride is hurt by telling another man how we have failed, even though we realize that a priest represents God Himself. But God demands that we confess our serious faults to His minister, partly because it would be too easy simply to say a possibly thoughtless "I'm sorry" in our hearts, quickly returning to commit the same sin again. Confessing to a priest and listening to his advice makes us think more seriously of what we have done.

Catholics tell a lot of humorous stories about confession. One of my favorites concerns the well-known former Governor of the State of New York, Alfred E. Smith. He was a pious man and went to confession at regular intervals, because people who are trying to deepen their love for God try to root out even little sins from their lives.

One day before Easter, large numbers of people were going to confession and Governor Smith was standing patiently in line awaiting his turn. There was finally only one little old lady ahead of him, who recognized him as the Governor. When it was her turn to enter the confessional, she looked over her shoulder and said:

"Governor Smith, you are a busy man, go in ahead of me."

"Madam," the Governor replied, "I insist that you precede me. I am in no more of a hurry to go in there than you are!"

Going to confession is akin to doing sitting-up exercises: no one really likes to do them, but one feels so much better after them. There is no contentment, there is no exhilaration so great as the peace and joy that floods the soul of one who confesses the errors of the past, receives forgiveness and promises sincerely to live better in the future.

Confession is far from being, as some critics of the past suggested, a license to sin. It is just the opposite. It is a new start on the road to virtue and, as Governor Smith realized, new starts are not easy, but one never progresses without making them.

The Holy Father has called this Holy Year, the Holy Year of Reconciliation. When we sin, we often offend both God and man and we should try to reconcile ourselves, to reestablish good relations with both God and our neighbor. It is not enough simply to say "I'm sorry," without making an effort to right the wrongs we have done, if possible, and to act justly toward our neighbor in the future.

Another reason that the Pope has chosen the theme of reconciliation for this Holy Year is because many people today have lost the sense of sin; they do not know, or at least will not admit, that they are doing wrong. One will never reform if one will not admit that one has done wrong. So when the Church calls on us to reconcile ourselves with our brothers and sisters, she is calling on us to admit the bad things we have done, to teach our consciences to be more sensitive to the difference between good and evil. As St. John the Evangelist said: "How can we love God whom we do not see, if we do not love our neighbor, whom we do see?" Wars, racial injustice, neglect of the poor, addiction to harmful substances, and so many human miseries are the result of personal sins of pride, greed, laziness, sensuality, and so forth. If everyone would recognize sin for what it is, if everyone would admit his guilt, if everyone would try to reform, what a pleasant world we could live in.

So you can see that the purpose of the Holy Door and the Holy Year is to serve mankind as well as worship God. God made His Church not to be served by mankind, but to serve mankind. The Church teaches men and women not for her own good, but for theirs. So if you see Catholics passing through the Holy Door of their own local cathedral or of St. Peter's in Rome, if you see them waiting patiently in line to go to confession, understand what they are trying to do. They are trying to create a better world by reconciling themselves with their Creator and with their fellow creatures, so that men and women will live together as brothers and sisters in peace and tranquillity as a foretaste of eternal life with God, which is to come.

The Respective Rights of the Family, Church and State in the Education of the Child

Address of Silvio Cardinal Oddi to the Michigan Chapter of Catholics United for the Faith, Detroit, Michigan, U.S.A., July 16, 1983.

My dear Brothers and Sisters in the Lord:

Apart from the Spanish Missions, I do not believe that there are many parts of present-day United States of America which can boast of a much earlier Catholic tradition than the State of Michigan, where St. Isaac Jogues preached to the Chippewas scarcely twenty years after the Pilgrims landed on Plymouth Rock. So it is, indeed, a spiritual joy for me to visit Michigan for the first time, and to discover for myself that the State, known the world over for its vast industrial production, is also a region of long and intensive Catholic life, a witness to which, too, is your presence here tonight.

I have long realized that underneath the enormous material prosperity of the United States—though I am aware, also, of people living in poverty among you—there is an unrivaled spiritual depth, which often is overlooked by some who call attention to your riches. So it gives me special pleasure to see with my own eyes the numbers drawn this evening by nothing other than a profound love for our common faith.

But I have not come here to embarrass your modesty with praise. I have been invited, as you know, to discuss a problem that is growing among you, a problem which is not new to the Church but which at times becomes more visible as the passing circumstances of history and contemporary thinking fluctuate. I refer to the problem of establishing a just balance between the educational rights and duties of the community of the family and of the larger communities of the Church and of the State in the education of children.

An element of this problem which is somewhat new today is the tension which can arise between the rights of the family and the rights and duties of local Church authorities in Christian education. This is a vast subject, and I am nervous even to bring it up in the short time we have available. But it is a grave and timely subject and must be faced. To begin, let us look briefly at the nature of the major educating communities which affect and form the child.

A community is a body of people having common goals, common organization and interests, and living in the same place under common rules. It takes little thought to realize that each of us and each child belongs to not one but to many communities: the family, the parish, the school, the scouts, the labor union, a political party, and so forth. Man and woman are social beings and not only prefer but need to live and work together in order to survive, even spiritually, because we cannot be saved alone, but only through the Church (Eph. 4:11-16; Acts 4:12).

Most communities are founded to achieve good purposes: to facilitate the realization of man's various legitimate desires for peace and tranquillity, for health, for culture, for comfort and, above all, for eternal happiness. But as the various communities pursue laudable goals, it is normal to experience that the rights of one community conflict with the rights of another. For example, a man has the right to enjoy good music. His neighbor has the right to peace and tranquillity. Problem: the first man's hi-fi disturbs the second man's quiet.

When we contemplate the education of the child, we are struck immediately by the large number of sometimes conflicting communities to which the child belongs and, therefore, by the large and varied number of people who contribute, for good or for ill, to his or her education: parents, siblings, priests, religious, neighbors, the Little League coach, teachers, scout masters and so forth. Some of these are minor figures in the child's life, whose rights evaporate when mother says, "No." But other community personages are not so easily dismissed—for example, the bishop, the pastor, the school principal—for the rights and obligations of all major communities must be harmonized in some way with the rights and obligations of the family itself.

Family: Domestic Sanctuary

In free countries, both Church and State recognize that the child's basic community is his or her family, because the family is the foundation stone of human society. Vatican Council II even calls the family the domestic church, explaining that "the mission of being the primary cell of society has been given to the family by God Himself," adding that it "presents itself as a domestic sanctuary[1] of the Church." The family is the chrysalis in which the child is first nurtured and eventually becomes a man or a woman. Both Church and State are defenders of the family because both Church[2] and State exist for man, or should.

The Founding Fathers of your own country declared that the State exists to serve man. Man does not exist to serve the State. They wrote in your famous "Declaration of

Independence" that "governments are instituted among men to secure these rights...of Life, Liberty and the Pursuit of Happiness." While the common good is also to be sought, it may not be purchased with the coin of violation of the rights of the individual. This is one of the reasons the State should oppose abortion and euthanasia.

Pope John Paul II insisted in his apostolic exhortation on the family that "the right and duty of parents to provide education [for their children] is an essential one, since it is connected with the transmission of human life; it is original and primary with respect to the educational role of others...it is irreplaceable and inalienable and, therefore, incapable of being entirely delegated to others or of being usurped by others."[3]

In saying this, the present Holy Father was simply repeating the long consistent teaching of the Church on this subject. Back in 1929, Pope Pius XI, for example, wrote that "the family,...therefore, holds directly from the Creator the mission and hence the right to educate the offspring; a right inalienable because it is joined inseparably to a strict obligation...and, therefore, inviolable by any power on earth."[4]

These principles apply, of course, not only to education offered by the State but also to religious education offered by the Church in parish schools, Christian doctrine classes and other educational centers for the young. Even in religious matters the parent retains the primary responsibility for the education of the child. Pope John Paul II teaches that "the State and the Church have the obligation to give families all possible *aid* to enable them to perform their educational role properly."[5] Note, he does not suggest that either Church or State usurp the parent's responsibility, rather they must both create and foster institutions and activities that families justly demand.

Bishop—First Teacher of Faith

I have no doubt that some of you will be very pleased to hear quoted the teachings of the Holy Father on the rights of parents in the education of their children. But, of course, the education of the child in today's world is a complicated process. First of all, parents are not the source of Christian doctrine. They themselves must know the teachings of Christ before they can pass them on to their children, and this is not always the case. In the realm of doctrine and morals the bishop is the first teacher in the diocese.[6] "Bishops are authentic teachers, that is, teachers endowed with the authority of Christ, who preach the faith to the people assigned to them, the faith which is destined to inform their thinking and direct their conduct." Secondly, every set of parents will have legitimate preferences on how their child should be educated, but, in parish or public schools enrolling several hundred children, there is a practical limit to the extent to which individual parental preferences can be honored, particularly since there can easily arise conflicts between the preferences of one family and those of another.

Does this mean that, in effect, present-day mass education requires by its nature that professional teachers take over completely the education of the child and that the parents, for the sake of efficiency and good organization, are called upon to abandon their child into the hands of the professionals, be they of the Church or State? By no means. Parents retain an active place in both the religious and the secular education of their children, for parents retain the right to be listened to, and they should insist that their right be respected.

The right to communicate their ideas is particularly valid when parents' common sense tells them that something is wrong. They must have the courage to stand up for their convictions. An obvious example of this right and obligation is the present trend in education in human sexuality. One does not need a doctorate in psychology to know that anything related to human sexuality is extremely provocative to adolescent boys and girls. This reaction has been given by the Creator to procure the survival of the human race. But God has endowed the young with a natural modesty, which is reinforced in a good home, to protect them from misusing their generative powers until they are old enough to use them legitimately and to provide for the education and support of the children God may send them. If a school or other educational center presumes to teach sexuality in a manner contrary to the moral common sense of parents, that strips away the instinctive, healthy personal modesty with which God endows youth, that suggests explicitly or by calculated omission that there is no right or wrong in any sexual conduct if enough individuals practice it, and that offers the same young people instruction on mechanical contraception and abortion as a remedy for sexual indulgence, then parents have not only the right but the duty to stand up and defend ethical sanity and Christian morality.

The Holy Father himself declared that "the Church is firmly opposed to an often widespread form of imparting sex education disassociated from moral principles.... Sex education, which is a basic right and duty of parents, must always be carried out under their attentive guidance, whether at home or in educational centers controlled by them."[7] Parents must be strong enough not to yield to the "experts" on these vital and delicate matters when their own intelligence tells them that the "experts" are wrong. I have the utmost respect for physical science and serious physical scientists, recently reinforced by a visit to your extraordinary National Air and Space Museum in Washington. But, on the other hand, I never fail to be amused by the cavalier manner in which some "experts" add or subtract millions of years to the age of man and seem to expect the man in the street to accept the new figure with hardly a hint that it may be wrong again.

Morality, Bad for the Health

An example of such scientific carelessness which led astray more than one generation is the recently publicized case of Margaret Mead. When a young anthropologist, she spent a short time on the Pacific Island of Samoa. Lacking the language, she depended on local interpreters. From her brief, second-hand study of local mores she came to the unshakable conclusion that there were no marital problems, psychological tensions, neurotic stress and so forth on that island precisely because the people practiced a sort of free love and were not constrained by Christian morality. In her widely read book,[8] she suggested that the western world, too, could escape the psychosomatic diseases plaguing it by abandoning its moral principles. In other words, the Ten Commandments were bad for the health.

Good parents instinctively knew that this made no sense whatsoever. But many of the educational "experts" sided with Dr. Mead. Recently, a half-century later, another anthropologist, Dr. Derek Freeman, has published his book on sexual attitudes in Samoa.[9] He speaks the language of the people and after years of study maintains that Samoans have high moral standards. Their moral code, in fact, censures pre-marital sexual relations and infidelity in marriage. So the whole factual foundation of Dr. Mead's bizarre theories, which pandered to the lower instincts of human nature, has been undermined. In the meantime, however, several generations have been affected by it, and one wonders whether the "experts" will be influenced by the new facts which offend their own preconceived ideas.

The point of all this is, of course, to urge parents not to doubt their own intelligence, simply because someone with a degree proposes a theory which goes contrary to common sense. I am *not* steering you toward obscurantism, nor toward closing your mind to legitimate new discoveries and developments, but what I am saying is that an academic degree, in any discipline, is not a guarantee of infallibility, particularly if the theory proposed offends our conscience.

The educational role of the parent begins long before the child reaches school. Even if the child is eventually sent to the best schools, these will not be able to make up for all he or she has missed, if his or her religious formation did not previously begin at home. There is a lot of talk these days about when and how a child's conscience matures. But parents I have talked to agree that the child begins to manifest an awareness of the difference between right and wrong from a very tender age. It is during these early months and years that the child should be taught patience, kindness, forgiveness, generosity, truthfulness, honesty and so forth, not only or even principally by word, but by example at home. The little mind should be taught specifically also about the spiritual world by those who brought the child into this one. How beautiful it is to see a parent or a grandparent teaching a youngster to make the Sign of the Cross, the Sign of the Trinity, to genuflect to the Blessed Sacrament, to dip the tiny hand in holy water, to answer grace at meals, to learn the Hail Mary. Every once in a while I see an adult lead a child around a church, pointing out the altar, the tabernacle lamp, the statues, the baptistry, the confessional. The child will never forget these early impressions, particularly when made on it by someone he or she loves and trusts. At difficult moments later in life those stained glass windows will return to mind, and clouds of adult problems will be dispelled by the rays of childhood memories.

First Confession

When the child approaches the age of reason, it has been the traditional practice of the Church since the time of Pope St. Pius X, who died just before the First World War, to lead the youngster to make his or her First Confession and First Communion. Before Pius X, as many of you will recall from studying Church history, the custom was to delay making one's First Communion until adolescence. But "The Pope of Little Children" welcomed little ones to the table of the Lord, as soon as they could distinguish between the Eucharist and ordinary bread.[10]

However, at the same time, he also called them to make their First Confession, to say "I'm sorry" to God. This saintly man certainly did not believe that seven or eight-year-old youngsters had fallen into serious sin and needed confession for their salvation. He was simply a good teacher, or a good spiritual parent, if you like. He wished to instill in their little minds the purity of soul with which Jesus should be received. He wished to start them early in the habit of making a confession of their sins, when it was easy because they had little to tell, just as good parents teach children as early as possible to look both ways before crossing the street. He wanted them to learn to confide their little worries to a priest, because he knew that in the sanctuary of the human conscience there are sometimes things that can be confided only to God, at whatever one's age. Parents must be careful to respect the sanctuary of their child's conscience.

At first this new sacramental freedom for children was joyously received by the Church and especially by children themselves. But recently this great sacramental favor is being denied to children in some areas. Children are being led to receive Our Lord in Holy Communion for the first time even before they have received the Sacrament of Penance. We are being told that children are traumatized by going to confession at the age of seven or eight. I celebrated my fiftieth anniversary of priesthood this year, and I have never met anyone who told me in any of the many countries in which I have heard confessions, that he or she was traumatized as a child by going to confession.

Some children these days seem to have more contact with the school psychologist than they have with their confessor. Do you think there is a connection? We see long lines of young people and adults going to Holy Communion, but the confessional lines have almost disappeared. It is possible that the recent denial to the child of First Confession before First Communion has only intensified the loss of a sense of sin among people of every generation.

Recently, Pope John Paul II told a group of American Bishops: "It is our role as Bishops to point out that both original sin and personal sin are at the basis of the sins that affect society"[11] and, I might add, that affect the family. If a child is not aware of sin, of having offended God, he or she is not even capable of saying the Hail Mary, let alone of desiring and working toward perfection.

Pope Pius X was a master of the human heart. He knew what he was doing, and the ordinary common sense of the average parent recognizes he was right and resists those who try to delay the First Confession of the child until after First Communion on the grounds of imagined fears born of secularistic principles. I fully agree that there could be occasional cases of children for whom First Confession around the time of reaching the use of reason would not be advisable. But exceptions only prove the rule, and it certainly does not conform to the spirit of the Church to make parents and children who follow the guidelines of Pope St. Pius X, of Paul VI and the present dispositions of the Holy See look like oddities, because certain "experts," religious or otherwise, have pronounced against the Holy See.

Contradiction

The question spontaneously arises at this point as to what parents can and should do when other communities to which the child is exposed or belongs contradict the formation which parents think their child should receive. When parents find themselves in disagreement with the formation their child is being given in any kind of school, the first thing they should do is think, research and pray over the problem themselves. Sometimes the first news parents have of a given school policy is not accurate. Their own child, or a neighbor, or a neighbor's child may have been misinformed. It is necessary to get the facts right. Then the parents should study the subject through reading, through reliable advisers, consulting, especially, a priest if it concerns faith and morals. Then it is necessary to pray, to try to look at the problem as God sees it and to beg His guidance.

In your country you have the laudable institution called "Parent-Teacher Associations." If the parents feel the problem needs airing before other parents and teachers, this would be an obvious forum in which to make their point of view known, and through which to discover what lies behind the practice or instruction which parents find harmful.

The new Code of Canon Law, which takes effect this coming Advent, obliges teachers to pay careful attention to parents: "It is necessary that parents cooperate closely with school teachers to whom they entrust their children to be educated; teachers, in turn, in fulfilling their obligations, should cooperate intimately with parents; parents should be listened to willingly, and associations of parents should be established which should be highly esteemed."[12]

If parents do not find the relief they seek from the school itself, they certainly have a right to speak with the pastor and with the Diocesan Chancery. Vatican Council II is quite clear about this in its instruction to Priests. The clergy are called upon "to listen to lay people, give brotherly consideration to their wishes, and recognize their experience and competence in the different fields of human activity."[13]

The Bishop is obviously the highest local Church authority to whom the faithful can appeal, and you people of Detroit are fortunate to have a zealous, faithful, apostolic, courageous Archbishop. He rules the diocese as a successor of the Apostles;[14] and as the Apostles were in communion with St. Peter, so the Archbishop of Detroit seeks to remain in close ecclesial communion with the rest of the Episcopal College and in particular manner with the Bishop of Rome.

Of course the Archbishop cannot handle all the work of a large diocese like Detroit by himself; he needs trusted collaborators who are in a position to speak for him, just as the Holy Father needs collaborators to conduct the business of the various offices of the Holy See. I have no doubt that the Archbishop of Detroit receives nearly as much mail, if not more, than I do in Rome at my post in the Sacred Congregation for the Clergy, which includes a desk for Catechetical Instruction. I try to answer every letter that comes in, but I admit that sometimes I fall behind if a letter writing campaign begins on a given problem. Some problems can be solved immediately. Others depend for solution on local circumstances which are sometimes difficult to adjust at a distance. Some complaints reject the practice of the Church or of the Holy See and neither the Bishop nor I can yield on those. Legitimate complaints are, however, given our serious attention.

In the field of catechesis both the Archbishop of Detroit and I realize that teaching is an art and artists like to do things their own way. The Church respects that legitimate individuality as long as the catechetical techniques employed are consonant with human dignity and the Church's own norms. So, while every teacher's pedagogical skills must be honored, the catechist must remain faithful to the Universal Magisterium of the Church.[15] The Local Church and the Universal Church must work together in these matters for there is in reality only One Church, and not many churches of Jesus Christ. The local Bishops and the Holy See constitute a single teaching authority.

Persistence is important, but so is courtesy, understanding, patience. Sometimes there are reasons why Church authorities must tolerate a given situation for a time because of circumstances, which it may be harmful to make public, and therefore a situation may remain unchanged and unexplained for an extended period. Parents should have confidence in their Bishops in such a state of affairs, protecting their own children as best they can, while remaining peaceful in their own conscience that they have fulfilled their obligation to open their mind and heart to the proper authorities. We live in an imperfect world but are strengthened by the conviction that God knows all secrets, those of everybody, and the deepest secrets eventually will be revealed (Mt. 10:26).

Of course, parents must be careful not to force their own preferences on others, with regard to questions about which legitimate pluralism may exist. The Apostles' Creed is fixed, it goes without saying, but in pastoral practice, in discipline, in certain aspects of worship, Vatican Council II has left many things either to the discretion of the National Bishops' Conference or to the local Bishop, and, in some cases, even to individual Priests according to the nature of the specific matter involved and local needs.[16]

On the other hand, the Holy Father recently warned that "it would be a grave error to set up pastoral requirements in opposition to doctrinal teaching, since the very first service that the Church must perform for people is to tell them *the truth,* of which the Church herself is neither the author nor the master."[17] Catholic teaching, for example, requires that a penitent confess his sins personally to a priest in ordinary circumstances, listen to eventual counsel from the priest and receive penance and absolution personally from that same priest. It would be a grave error to impart general absolution to satisfy invented pastoral needs, thereby distorting the deposit of truth over which the Church herself has no authority.

Just as there is no magic, infallible formula for raising children, so there is no magic, ready formula for obtaining cooperation among all the communities which contribute to the integral formation of the child. But one thing is certain: the good of the child is paramount and must be the measuring rod for parents, for Church and State. Jesus excluded no one when He warned, "Whoever causes one of these little ones who believe in me to sin, it would be better for him to have a great millstone fastened around his neck and to be drowned in the depths of the sea" (Mt. 18:6).

When the real good of the child is procured, so also is the good of the Church achieved. If the communities involved realize that their own good cannot be separated from the good of the child, they will find themselves working in concert. Individual initiatives may be good in themselves, but it is the child's good we should be seeking, not personal satisfaction. This is why the Holy Father recently declared on his trip to Nicaragua: "The unity of the Church can only be saved when each one is capable of giving up his own ideas, plans and commitments—even good ones—for the greater good of communion with the Bishops, with the Pope."[18]

There is a God in Heaven Who knows all and Whose divine life fills the hearts of those who are in the state of grace. So, while not seeking escape into a pusillanimous quietism, neither should we be tempted to think that everything must be done by us personally. When decisions are difficult, when one is not sure which way to turn, pray, pray often, pray fervently, for your faith can move mountains (cf. Mt. 21:21). Remember that while "Paul plants and Apollos waters, it is God who gives the increase" (1 Cor. 3:6). Given their diversity of composition and sometimes even their divergence in principles and purpose, it is, in the last analysis, only God Who can move all the communities which influence a child to work in harmony for the child's good.

NOTES

1. Vatican Council II, Decree *Apostolicam actuositatem*, no. 11.

2. Pope John Paul II, Encyclical *Redemptor hominis*, no. 14, 1979.

3. Pope John Paul II, Encyclical *Familiaris consortio*, no. 36, 1981.

4. Pope Pius XI, Encyclical *Divini illius magistri*, 1929 *(AAS* 1930, pp. 49-86).

5. *Familiaris consortio*, no. 40.

6. Vatican Council II, Constitution *Lumen gentium*, no. 25.

7. *Familiaris consortio*, no. 37.

8. Mead, Margaret, *Coming of Age in Samoa* (Morrow), 1928.

9. Freeman, Derek, *Margaret Mead and Samoa. The Making and Unmaking of an Anthropological Myth*. Harvard Univ. Press, 1983.

10. Pope St. Pius X, Decree *Quam singulari*, 1910 *(AAS* 1910, pp. 577-583).

11. Pope John Paul II, Address to the Bishops of the Metropolitan Province of New York on their *ad limina* visit, April 15, 1983, no. 4 (English ed. of *L'Osservatore Romano*, April 25, 1983, p. 6).

12. Code of Canon Law, 1983, can. 796.

13. Vatican Council II, Decree *Presbyterorum ordinis*, no. 9.

14. *Lumen gentium*, no. 18.

15. Vatican Council II, Decree *Christus Dominus*, no. 14.

16. *Lumen gentium*, no. 23.

17. Pope John Paul II, Address to the First Plenary Assembly of the Pontifical Council for the Family, May 30, 1983, no. 4 (English ed. of *L'Osservatore Romano*, June 6, 1983, p. 7).

18. Pope John Paul II, Address on visit to Managua, Nicaragua, March 4, 1983, no. 5 (English ed. *L'Osservatore Romano* March 28, 1983, p. 6).

Catechetical Source Material

FOR CATHOLIC SCHOOLS
AND CCD PROGRAMS
THE TWO ST. PAUL RELIGION SERIES
FOR INTEGRAL
CHRISTIAN DEVELOPMENT

THE WAY, TRUTH AND LIFE SERIES

1 GOD THE FATHER SENT HIS SON
The salvation message—an encounter with Jesus.

2 CHRIST LIVES IN ME
God's life in us—Baptism, Penance, Communion.

3 CHRIST, OUR WAY TO THE FATHER
Jesus, the Son of God—we imitate Jesus.

4 CHRIST'S LAW OF LOVE
Our Christian responsibilities: Commandments, Beatitudes, Special duties of Catholics.

5 ALIVE IN THE SPIRIT
The Church and the Sacraments.

6 LIVE THE MASS
Our relationship with Jesus grows through Eucharistic Celebration.

7 HIS SAVING LOVE
God's love shown through the Old and New Testaments.

8 LIVE THE TRUTH! GIVE THE TRUTH!
Knowing, living and sharing our Faith.

TEXTBOOKS, ACTIVITY BOOKS, TEACHER'S MANUALS AND PARENT'S GUIDES are available for each grade.
   Complete catalog and Scope and Sequence Chart available on request.

The WAY, TRUTH and LIFE Series is also available in a SPANISH/ENGLISH EDITION.

Programs are also available for Pre-School, Preparation for First Penance and First Communion, Confirmation, and Adult Religious Education. Please write for more information.

THE DIVINE MASTER SERIES

is a flexible, stimulating program for CCD or parochial schools. The texts normally used in the Divine Master CCD program are:

9 MASTER PLAN REVEALED
How can I witness to Christ? Stresses: character and personality; God as known through reason and revelation; and the life of Christ.

10 THE CHURCH'S AMAZING STORY
(Second Semester)
A readable "biography" of the Church and her great sons and daughters. A best seller!

10 GOD'S PEOPLE ON THE MOVE
(First Semester)
The Holy Spirit working through the Church today.

11 REALLY LIVING
The Commandments as a sign of our love and a practical guide to Christian living.

12 LOOKING AHEAD TO MARRIAGE
A comprehensive and enjoyable marriage course.

AN ENLARGED DIVINE MASTER HIGH SCHOOL SERIES is also available for use in Catholic high school religion programs, as well as a number of additional electives.
Teacher's manuals available for each text.
Please write for more information.

Answers to Your Questions—Rev. Richard V. Lawlor, S.J.

There is no problem that faith cannot solve, no question that truth cannot answer. This timely volume contains inquiries sent in by readers of *The Family* magazine over a period of several years.

Covering topics such as prayer, morals, doctrine, marriage, ethics, and the Bible, a competent theologian provides in a concise but clear manner answers to *your* questions. This book is a helpful guide in confronting the prominent issues of our day—a book of answers in an age of questioning. 216 pages—RA0005

Apostolic Exhortation on Catechesis in Our Time
(Catechesi Tradendae)—Pope John Paul II

The mission of handing on the Catholic Faith is presented clearly in this document of Pope John Paul II, emphasizing Jesus Christ, the heart of catechesis; the need of catechesis today; catechesis from the time of the Apostles; what is to be included in catechesis; the aim, ways and means of catechesis, and more. This is an excellent guide for every teacher of catechesis and every parent, as well as priests and bishops. 67 pages—EP0185

Basic Catechism—Daughters of St. Paul

This concise, direct book presents the fundamentals of the Catholic Faith in a question-and-answer format with related scriptural quotations.

Thoroughly indexed for ready reference, it is a vital handbook for anyone desiring to deepen or clarify his belief. 208 pages—RA0007

Teacher's Manual for Basic Catechism
Daughters of St. Paul

Two separate manuals to accompany *Basic Catechism*. They provide ample material to help any teacher communicate the Faith. Grades one through six—RA0007E; grades seven through twelve—RA0007H

A Brief Summary of the Ten Commandments
Daughters of St. Paul

A theological question-and-answer treatment. Complete with scriptural facts and Vatican II pastoral teachings. 96 pages—CA0200

Catechism for Adults—Rev. James Alberione, SSP, STD

Theology at your fingertips. This volume clearly and concisely offers answers to the questions the man of today is asking. Ideal for individual reading, convert instruction classes, and discussion groups. 272 pages—RA0010

The Catechism of Modern Man—Edited and Compiled by a team of Daughters of St. Paul

Best Seller

Over 9,000 topics—*The Catechism of Modern Man* is the only complete source of the Council's new and profound expression of the Faith—all in the words of Vatican II and related post-conciliar documents. 731 pages—RA0020

Christ in Catechesis—Daughters of St. Paul

Our youth today need a firm foundation in their Faith in order to face the inevitable challenges life presents, and religious instruction should provide that basis necessary for our young people to live the Christian life to their full spiritual advantage.

Christ in Catechesis applies a spirituality centered on Jesus, the Way, Truth and Life, to catechetics and opens new horizons to all involved in religious education.

The Way, Truth and Life method presented in these pages can form the students—mind, will and heart—in Christ, and bring them to a deeper knowledge of the Person of Jesus Christ and His teachings as handed down to us by His Church. Evidenced in these pages are the constant concern and timeless response of the Church to the needs of all who seek to live a truly Christian life.

Christ in Catechesis is a necessary and excellent guide for all involved in the education and formation of youth. 120 pages—RA0053

The Eternal Wisdom—Rev. James Alberione, SSP, STD

Often called a one-book encyclopedia of the Catholic Faith—a brilliant four-color art master accompanies each page of explanation with Scripture references throughout. An ideal family book and convert manual. 180 pages—RA0090

"Going, Teach..."—Commentary on the Apostolic Exhortation *Catechesi Tradendae* of Pope John Paul II

Coordinator: Cesare Bonivento, PIME; Edited by the Institute of Missionary Catechesis; Translated by Daughters of St. Paul

In more than 600 pages, 40 specialists give a commentary on the Apostolic Exhortation of Pope John Paul II on *Catechesis in Our Time*.

Contains the complete text of *Catechesi tradendae*, and an index of the commentary. 728 pages—RA0114

Morality Today—The Bible in My Life
Daughters of St. Paul

A unique way to study the ten commandments!

In simple and clear language, but with a very personal approach, each commandment is explained in all its aspects, negative and positive. We are invited to ponder...adore...and speak to God so that through instruction, reflection and prayer we may understand and love His holy law.

All will find this book both informative and inspirational.
167 pages—SC0088

Religion for People of Today—Daughters of St. Paul

Squarely facing the questions everyone is asking in these days of confusion, this concise religious instruction book speaks modern man's language. Solid in its doctrine, contemporary in its presentation, it will prove ideal for adult discussion groups, classes or individual reading. 112 pages—RA0150

St. Paul Family Catechism—Daughters of St. Paul
Introduction by Most Rev. Pio Laghi,
Apostolic Delegate to the U.S.A.

878 questions and answers and a detailed index!

"The Daughters of St. Paul are to be commended for the publication of their *St. Paul Family Catechism*. This invaluable catechetical tool, modeled after the great catechisms that have been a part of the Catholic Church's tradition, will enable parents to meet their educational responsibilities more effectively" (from the Introduction). 392 pages—CA0500

Mount St. Mary's Seminary
Emmitsburg, MD 21727

December 21, 1983

Dear Sisters,

I just finished reading your new Family Catechism. It impressed me so much that I couldn't resist sending you a note of congratulations. I especially like your clear, up-to-date, and concise treatment of moral theology, including current issues like euthanasia, sexual ethics, and fundamental option.

I only wish that I had been able to use the new catechism two years ago when I was teaching CCD. It would have helped enormously. I'm very glad to have it now and I'll recommend it to others, particularly parents. Also I found it to be good spiritual reading since it provides a beautiful and simple view of our whole Faith. It's refreshing to sit down for a few hours and read the simple truth that so many Catholics before us have been so fortunate to know and love and hand on to others.

Good work, sisters! And thank you for all your fine work!

In Christ,
Michael Kerper, Seminarian

Spiritual Life in the Bible—Daughters of St. Paul

A volume which pursues the truth about a wealth of timely and fundamental subjects.

Written in a form of dialogue, the author continually draws from the Book of books—the Bible—whose Author is God, the Author of Truth and the true Light of the world.

A book which will be of interest to both those who believe in objective truth, and those who honestly seek to pursue the truth.
456 pages—SC0445

Symposium on the Magisterium: A Positive Statement—Edited by Msgr. John J. O'Rourke and S. Thomas Greenburg

A positive response to the continuing debate about the Magisterium, its meaning, composition, authority and proper function. Among those taking part in the symposium were Cardinal Krol of Philadelphia, Archbishop Whealon of Hartford, Bishop Maloney, Abbot McCaffrey, and others. 152 pages—RA0185

The Teaching Church in Our Time
Edited by George A. Kelly

Covers the relationship to the magisterium of Catholic doctrine in the following areas—Scripture, Tradition, modernism, infallibility, catechetics and sexual matters. The contributors are Msgr. Eugene Kevane; Fr. Manuel Miguens, OFM; Fr. Robert Bradley, SJ; Fr. John Hardon, SJ; Fr. Joseph Hogan, CM; Fr. Bruce A. Williams, OP; all faculty members of the Institute for Advanced Studies in Catholic Doctrine at St. John's University, New York City. 250 pages—RA0190

Vatican Council II—The Conciliar and Post-Conciliar Documents (2 Volumes)
General Editor—Austin Flannery, OP

"The need for the book is crucial, not only for readers of English, but for scholars generally.... The compendium is a unique collection of translations into English of Council documents, together with selected subsequent Roman documents which amplify, elucidate, or apply the major themes of the Vatican Council constitutions, decrees and other major pronouncements..." (John Cardinal Wright).
Volume 1, 1062 pages—EP1097; Volume 2, 926 pages—EP1101

Daughters of St. Paul

MASSACHUSETTS
 50 St. Paul's Ave., Jamaica Plain, Boston, MA 02130; **617-522-8911**.
 172 Tremont Street, Boston, MA 02111; **617-426-5464; 617-426-4230**.

NEW YORK
 78 Fort Place, Staten Island, NY 10301; **212-447-5071; 212-447-5086**.
 59 East 43rd Street, New York, NY 10017; **212-986-7580**.
 625 East 187th Street, Bronx, NY 10458; **212-584-0440**.
 525 Main Street, Buffalo, NY 14203; **716-847-6044**.

NEW JERSEY
 Hudson Mall—Route 440 and Communipaw Ave.,
 Jersey City, NJ 07304; **201-433-7740**.

CONNECTICUT
 202 Fairfield Ave., Bridgeport, CT 06604; **203-335-9913**.

OHIO
 2105 Ontario Street (at Prospect Ave.), Cleveland, OH 44115;
  216-621-9427.
 25 E. Eighth Street, Cincinnati, OH 45202; **513-721-4838; 513-421-5733**.

PENNSYLVANIA
 1719 Chestnut Street, Philadelphia, PA 19103; **215-568-2638**.

VIRGINIA
 1025 King Street, Alexandria, VA 22314; **703-683-1741; 703-549-3806**.

FLORIDA
 2700 Biscayne Blvd., Miami, FL 33137; **305-573-1618**.

LOUISIANA
 4403 Veterans Memorial Blvd., Metairie, LA 70002; **504-887-7631;
  504-887-0113**.
 1800 South Acadian Thruway, P.O. Box 2028, Baton Rouge, LA 70821;
  504-343-4057; 504-381-9485.

MISSOURI
 1001 Pine Street (at North 10th), St. Louis, MO 63101; **314-621-0346;
  314-231-1034**.

ILLINOIS
 172 North Michigan Ave., Chicago, IL 60601; **312-346-4228; 312-346-3240**.

TEXAS
 114 Main Plaza, San Antonio, TX 78205; **512-224-8101; 512-224-0938**.

CALIFORNIA
 1570 Fifth Ave., San Diego, CA 92101; **619-232-1442**.
 46 Geary Street, San Francisco, CA 94108; **415-781-5180**.

WASHINGTON
 2301 Second Ave., Seattle, WA 98121.

HAWAII
 1143 Bishop Street, Honolulu, HI 96813; **808-521-2731**.

ALASKA
 750 West 5th Ave., Anchorage, AK 99501; **907-272-8183**.

CANADA
 3022 Dufferin Street, Toronto 395, Ontario, Canada.

ENGLAND
 199 Kensington High Street, London W8 63A, England.
 133 Corporation Street, Birmingham B4 6PH, England.
 5A-7 Royal Exchange Square, Glasgow G1 3AH, England.
 82 Bold Street, Liverpool L1 4HR, England.

AUSTRALIA
 58 Abbotsford Rd., Homebush, N.S.W. 2140, Australia.